THE PRODIGAL FAMILY

THE PRODIGAL FAMILY

A Practical Guide for Family Forgiveness

T̄

Johanna Maaghul

For information on placing bulk orders for this book please contact:

Clear Lantern Media
72 Fresh Pond Parkway
Cambridge, MA 02138
http://www.theprodigalfamily.com

Cover design by Blaise Auberson

ISBN-10: 1449504248
ISBN-13: 978-1449504243

This book is dedicated to all the sons and daughters
trying to find their way back home.

Contents

And he said, "There was a man who had two sons.
And the younger of them said to his father,
'Father, give me the share of property that is coming to me.'
And he divided his property between them.
Not many days later, the younger son gathered
All he had and took a journey into a far country,
And there he squandered his property in reckless living.
And when he had spent everything, a severe famine arose in that country,
And he began to be in need.
So he went and hired himself out to one of the citizens of that country,
Who sent him into his fields to feed pigs.
And he was longing to be fed with the pods that the pigs ate,
And no one gave him anything.
But when he came to himself, he said,
'How many of my father's hired servants have more than enough bread,
But I perish here with hunger!
I will arise and go to my father, and I will say to him,
"Father, I have sinned against heaven and before you.
I am no longer worthy to be called your son.
Treat me as one of your hired servants."
And he arose and came to his father.
But while he was still a long way off, his father saw him and felt compassion,
And ran and embraced him and kissed him.
And the son said to him, 'Father, I have sinned against heaven and before you.
I am no longer worthy to be called your son.'
But the father said to his servants, 'Bring quickly the best robe,
And put it on him, and put a ring on his hand, and shoes on his feet.
And bring the fattened calf and kill it, and let us eat and celebrate.
For this my son was dead, and is alive again; he was lost, and is found.'
And they began to celebrate.

Now his older son was in the field, and as he came and drew near to the house,
He heard music and dancing. And he called one of the servants
And asked what these things meant. And he said to him,
'Your brother has come, and your father has killed the fattened calf,
Because he has received him back safe and sound.'
But he was angry and refused to go in. His father came out and entreated him,
but he answered his father, 'Look, these many years I have served you,
And I never disobeyed your command, yet you never gave me a young goat,
That I might celebrate with my friends. But when this son of yours came,

Who has devoured your property with prostitutes, you killed the fattened calf for him!'

And he said to him, 'Son, you are always with me, and all that is mine is yours. It was fitting to celebrate and be glad, for this your brother was dead, and is alive; He was lost, and is found.'

Luke 15:11–32

Acknowledgements

Writing this book has been a journey into the unknown for me – a journey I would not have been able to complete without the unyielding love, patience and encouragement of my husband, Rich, and my three amazing children, David, Olivia and Phillip. I cannot thank them enough for allowing me the space and time to unravel this new part of myself – all the time they gave me during family weekends, late nights, early mornings and all the moments in between when 'mom was busy with her book.'

The birth of this book began with the Christmas gift of an iPod, which I received for Christmas in 2006. Little did I know the impact that small device would have on me, my family, and the direction of my life. After my treatment for breast cancer, and while returning to my work as a computer programmer, I would listen to my iPod for hours as I absorbed interviews, discussions and thought provoking dialogues around issues of healing, consciousness and self discovery. During my audio journeys, I discovered and have since become acquainted with many wonderful teachers and guides who have been instrumental in the birth, transformation and completion of this book.

Thank you also to Cheryl Nelson who has been my sounding board and provided me with endless hours of conversation on what family healing really means. Molly Erker, my RCIA sponsor and friend, for challenging me to write. David Ord for his encouragement in the vision and mission of this book. Dee Wallace for her publishing wisdom. John Nelson and Pam Suwinsky for their diligent, thoughtful and honest editing. My parents for providing me with this adventure and to all the friends and family who have bravely recounted to me their own stories of separation and healing which have served as the inspiration for this book.

Preface

In the Spring of 2008, after more than twenty years of being away from the Catholic Church, my husband, Rich, made his first confession.

After his confession, we met at a small café in the city near our church. He shared with me the many moments of sin or of "missing the mark" he had chosen to bring into the light in the two decades that had passed. He took full responsibility, not in a general "Okay, I screwed up" way, but in the laser-focused "Here are all the things I did" way that he is known for. He amazes me with his ability to look inside and see himself in a way few of us are capable of, let alone have the courage to take on.

His "penance," as it were, was one simple request from the priest: to read the parable of the prodigal son. I had heard of the story but never read it. The more I pondered it, the more I came to understand its real message. We are all capable of falling off track when what we are doing no longer supports us or those around us in a healthy way. But what became clearer to me as I contemplated the prodigal son was that by taking this journey, he was able to find his way home, not just in the physical sense but in his ability to become a mature grown-up human being.

Reflecting on the story of the prodigal son has served as a reminder to me of the way in which I have lived much of my own life. As if in a dark room surrounded by all the spirits of my ancestors, I continue to reach for the light switch. Shedding the light onto what has been left for so long in the darkness has become my life's work, from which the stories and exercises in this book have been born. My own healing has been a work in progress, but each day that I can wake up and experience myself and my family with a sense of enthusiasm and joy is a day that the lights get turned on. I am still often left in the dark with the voices of my early years reminding me of my limits, but even those voices I am learning to make peace with — letting them coexist with my newly found grown-up self — the way we would let a small child learn to pick herself up from a fall, skinned knees and all.

How to Use This Book

The mission of this book is to help guide you through a new way of looking at family and to create a new *intention* for relating to your family members —not so much in your interactions with them, but in the dialogue that exists within your own mind and heart. By looking at our own internal discussion with our family — which we can carry on for years and years, even after we no longer live with them — we can loosen our tight grip on how we see them, make room for forgiveness, and possibly build new relationships with them.

Most important, however, I recommend that as you read through the ideas, stories, and exercises in this book, you continue to listen closely to your heart. Pay attention to your feelings of anxiety, sadness, anger, and disappointment, and whenever possible, let yourself experience and look at these feelings without judgment. Imagine that whatever feelings you have are probably not yours alone, but have been handed down over generations and may be shared by other family members. Your gift is in seeing them within the context, patterns, and story from which they came and by doing so setting yourself, your ancestors, and future generations free from the destiny of a family unfulfilled.

The themes and stories used in this book, particularly the story of the prodigal son and the images of the five circles explained in chapter two, should offer some new ways of viewing family relationships and how important love, forgiveness and humility are as ingredients in family healing. The letter-writing exercises in chapter six provide an opportunity to take some of these new concepts and apply them should you feel ready to reach out to family members in your own healing process. It is recommended that this book is read in the order in which it was written to make the most of how its message is presented.

Introduction

The story of the prodigal son provides a powerful illustration of a true passage through adolescence, which serves as the portal for all individuals as they move from childhood to adulthood. When we are not able to complete the cycle of adolescence during our normal adolescent years, we are not allowed to take the journey to find our own identity and *to grow up*. When we are raised by parents who also have not had the chance to become their own grown-up selves, our most challenging moments in life may not be our experiences in the outside world but instead the ones we face when we are trying to find the courage to be ourselves within our childhood home.

The Four Guiding Principles of Family Healing

In the process of writing this book, I spent time reflecting on my own life story, and in doing so arrived at a set of four guiding principals that I believe apply to the journey of family healing and self-discovery:

1. *We must take no prisoners.*

    The journey of family healing must be travelled by each individual member. One of my questions when writing this book was how much of my own family's history to share. It has been colorful, to say the least, but I veer from the track when I begin to focus on them and their role in my life rather than on the big picture of how the story of my family has helped me grow into who I was meant to be.

    I am acutely aware of the expression "The truth shall set you free," but I am also not oblivious to the fact that each person who has *apparently* betrayed or hurt me in my own family is on his or her own journey. Whenever I would catch myself getting stuck or spinning on a story or issue with a particular family member, I knew that it was a sign to let it go. Most likely I was still looking for something from that person, and it would not serve to drag you as the reader into the middle of it. I can take what each person has taught me on my journey, but much of the details of the story I must leave where they belong, in the past.

We in the end must make this journey alone. Our family members may be here to help shape who we are and find our real essence, but we, too, are characters in their stories as well.

2. *We must heal around that which cannot be healed.*

Forgiveness is the holy grail of all healing. There can be no healing in families if we are waiting for things to change. In sharing the ideas of this book with one of the guides on my own journey, I was reminded that the message I have to share is that *real healing occurs when we are willing to heal in spite of that which cannot be healed.* We must take all of the fodder from our family history, our ancestral lineage, and find a way to make sense of it, its patterns and lessons, and use these lessons to transform ourselves on our own hero's journey. If we can look back without judgment and take what we find when we call up the lost and buried treasures that were neglected during what may have been centuries of ancestral strife, we can begin to make whole not only ourselves, but our ancestral spirits, and, most important, our children for generations to come.

3. *Each of us is on our own hero's journey – even within our family.*

Grownups make the best parents, and if you have not had a chance to grow up yourself, you will inevitably be limited and less available to parent your own children. If you are reading this book, you have certainly been called to face this challenge and opportunity, and most likely you were not given a chance to pass through the gateway of adolescence in an appropriate and meaningful way in your own childhood. The hero's journey, as defined by Joseph Campbell in his work *The Power of Myth,* always includes a separation, a transformation (or initiation), and a reintegration. This process, once recognized in the events of your own life, can provide a healthy passage into adulthood, a second chance, so to speak, to gain what was not realized in a chronological adolescence. The hero's journey asks us to answer the call. By recognizing the hero's journey in your own life, you can begin to see the gifts you have been endowed with. It is your chance to discover yourself as the grownup you never had a chance to become and surrender your role as your parent's child.

4. *We are not immune to our environment.*
As much as humans would like to believe we are separate from nature, the breakdown, particularly in the United States, of our relationship with nature, our local tribes, indigenous cultures, and extended families has proved to have had an unavoidable ripple effect on the stability and balance of raising families today. A family is like an ecosystem; when any of its nurturing elements are disturbed or disrupted, the entire system can be thrown off balance. Moving from our country of origin, away from familiar food, relatives, friends, even the climate our bodies are the most comfortable in, can cause subtle yet profound changes in our ability to maintain balance within our family. As David Berceli points out in his book, *The Revolutionary Trauma Release Process*, family abuse in most cases can be traced back to a social trauma such as war, famine, or natural disaster from generations past. What is absorbed from the outside culture in one family may take generations before it is transformed into a family turned inward and resurfaces as a toxic force let loose on the family itself. In a culture where moving away from our homeland has become commonplace, it does not seem strange that raising a family has become a lonely and stressful task.

These four principals are applied throughout the stories and exercises in this book to remind us that although we are held in a physical reality as it relates to what we have been raised with in our life, we also hold the promise of infinite possibilities when we can find true acceptance in what has been and find very real ways to move beyond these limitations both physically and emotionally through committing ourselves to humility and forgiveness.

The story of the prodigal son is a story of forgiveness, a story of coming home, but it is also a story of growing up. When we make the space in our lives and remove ourselves from the shackles of our

7

relentless and constant self-criticism, we may find gifts that can create a new and more meaningful culture and way of being for our family for generations to come.

1. The Nuclear Family

Once upon a time there was a nuclear family,
And we lived in a family time,
And we'd unite in a family way.
And off in the ancient mountain,
They were splitting every nucleus.
They said, "Don't be alarmed,
Just don't try this at home."

— Dar Williams, *The Great Unknown*

I have been fascinated with math and geometry since I was a child. I had been a silent witness to my parents' divorce, and my fascination with math and science did not come without a cause. I worked hard to solve the psychological and emotional mysteries that were unfolding around me at an exponential rate. At the first breaking of the atom of my parents' divorce, I saw a new family culture being set into action — an ever-accelerating reality of *"every man, woman, and child for themselves"* – with each family member becoming more and more isolated and less and less able to give and connect to one another. The core energy field had been altered such that not only were the circles that contained and nurtured the family out of balance, but much of the structure, where a whole sphere of togetherness had once been, had been blown apart into tiny pieces of shrapnel.

The task of trying to see through the thick and disfigured membrane of what was once "our family" was my first calling on my own journey of self-discovery. With a deep propensity for mathematics at a very young age, I began trying to solve for *x*. There was not a day that went by that I did not contemplate the breakdown of human relationships.

I spent years as a teenager and young adult devouring any self-help and psychology books I could get my hands on, trying to find the set of tweezers with which I could extract the shrapnel from my skin, to see if there was any way I could get out of this alive, intact, and emotionally whole, and all the while find the formula to put the atom back together. The *real* problem, however, was that I did not have all of the data to solve the equation. In fact, what I failed to understand at the time was that *the single act of my parents' divorce was not a singular act at all. It was the cumulative quantum explosion of each of my parents' unique family histories — their own physical and emotional traumas being played out with each other again and again and finally creating enough friction to cause the big bang that was their divorce.*

If we, like the prodigal son, receive the call to be drawn away and out of our home of origin, we must be aware that what we return to after our transformation will be vastly different than what we originally were called away from. *We cannot assume that the man the prodigal son came home to was the same father that he left years before.* We must understand that *both* of their hearts had shifted in ways that could make way for the complete forgiveness of one another as well as of the past sins of generations.

Alone We Stand

For to stay, though the hours burn in the night,
Is to freeze and crystallize and be bound in a mould.
Fain would I take with me all that is here. But how shall I?
A voice cannot carry the tongue and the lips that give it wings.
Alone must it seek the ether.
And alone and without his nest shall the eagle fly across the sun.

- Kahlil Gibran, *The Prophet*

We are born into the world alone. We are birthed from our mother with nothing other than our physical body and our true essence. Had the development of our most true and authentic self been consistently nurtured during our childhood and adolescent years, we would in our adult life resonate and become a practitioner of our most gifted self.

For most of us, in American culture today, this is hardly the case. In our aloneness, we may have realized that our own parents did not have the chance to find their way to adulthood and are trapped in their own adolescence — still trying to find *themselves* in the later years of their lives.

The resulting family story may very well provide us with fertile ground for understanding and separating from what is not our true nature, but what is instead projected onto us out of the need to maintain control and continuity in the family — or as Don Miguel Ruiz states in his book, *The Four Agreements*, the family environment where we are first domesticated.

As we wade through our early years under such circumstances, we are confronted from the very beginning with the forces that challenge our sense of self. These forces may cause us great pain and distress as we try, while finding our own way in the world, to preserve our natural connection with our own spirit, our "higher power," or our life source energy and all that is good within us. These gifts and ways of being were our birthright; we came equipped with them when we arrived, but for many of us, it was not safe to keep them at the forefront of our day-to-day existence.

As children, we are acutely aware of the power our elders hold in our survival. In many situations, it would be futile if not dangerous for us to challenge this. As Carolyn Myss describes in her audio publication, *Self Esteem*, it is this lack of trust in our sense of self that keeps us loyal to our family code:

When a person lacks a sense of self, that person is not strong enough to hold the memories of an experience so the memories are contained within the tribal or the family collective. So when a child, for example, goes to a parent and says uncle is doing that to me or the neighbor is doing that to me, and let's say it brings on tribal shame to the self esteem of the tribe, the family or the tribe cannot afford to hear that — does not want that shame brought about or brought to the dignity of the whole therefore the self esteem of that one member is sacrificed to protect the self esteem of the whole. And in the process of that, the elders have made a decision out of elder wisdom that says this would destroy US so we cannot allow you, the individual, to harm US, and that's the way it is.

What happens is often is that the individual, its like a spell is cast, and that person says, well maybe it never happened, ok, right it never happened …your right it never happened, your right I was a bad little girl or bad little boy. You start doing something because your inner self very much knows that there has been a violation. What happens is …how you have met yourself on the road of "wound" — your immediate instinct is to recognize that. And often times when the self says I don't fit in the collective anymore, its time for me to go — what is your indicator is that you need to start with healing…

The self births itself in a birth canal and it's though the birth pains …and your psyche says its time to be born and I have to give you some birth pains and then you have to get through the canal of the tribal canal and form, discover and birth the self. Now that process is incredibly vulnerable because as you come into the self you inherently know your life is going to change. You have to change the rules. [1]

In this dramatic illustration, Myss describes the deep collective response to shame that is typical in families — the need to keep the lights turned off in the house for fear that the neighbors may see what is happening and could never possibly understand. The unraveling of such events is typical of many families who carry deep, untold stories — stories that may be reenacted over many generations, in which the acting out may change in subtle ways but continues to carry the belief that the story is too dark and disfigured to be exposed to the light.

---

[1] Quote from Carolyn Myss audio, *Self Esteem*, http://www.myss.com

As such stories and behaviors are passed down, the elders may be compelled to keep the behavior of the outspoken child in line with the rest of the tribe in an effort to thwart the anxiety of their own domestication — *as they still carry and repress unconscious rage at their own elders who had successfully domesticated them.* Our innocence, vibrancy, and free self-expression as a child can serve as unconscious and painful reminders to our elders of what has been lost on their own journey. As a result, we are relegated to a world of not only domestication but of *split realities* — one in which we exist alone and one in which we exist collectively with our family within the body of our false self.

For me, this splitting occurred as a result of spending far too much time on my own at a young age. At thirteen, I had already developed an empty hole in my heart where love and the connection to friends and family were meant to be. I can remember at this tender age building a makeshift cabin for myself over the creek behind our house. After hauling all of my clothing, my guitar, and most of my books down to the ten-by-ten foot shelter, I spent the summer living there, playing my guitar and reading. Looking back, is it clear to me that those who were meant to be nurturing me during these years were consumed by the adolescent role in their *own* lives, trying desperately to slow the clock and rebuild lost years for themselves, creating and recreating their own makeshift shelters — trying to find their own true path on their journey.

Ultimately, it wasn't until my early forties and my call to confront my diagnosis of breast cancer that I began to understand how deep the well of my own self-abandonment ran. Decades had passed for me, and I had hardly birthed the real person I was until it was demanded of me from the months of chemotherapy. As I began to flirt with the idea of letting this deeper self surface, I became frightened by the realization that I had built up around me deeply protective layers of false self. As I began to let my authentic self poke through, I was quickly dashed back by the "tribe" from which I came. Like a Greek chorus in a unified song, my family fought back my rebirth in ways so subtle I was not even sure of the changes or what I was trying to share with them. But I began to rethink my childhood experience and the baggage I was no longer willing to carry. I began to see the irony of the childhood experience as I formulated the following thought:

For many, the "family" experience of childhood or growing up becomes a cruel joke. The entire model, which all of our folklore and culture pitches to us as a world bathed in "togetherness" becomes one of the loneliest phases of time spent on Earth. During this time, many of us learn to both question those who have been entrusted to care for us and to remain infinitely loyal and true to them and the code that we are raised with. It is in this duality that we eventually learn to live — relegating our true selves to our deepest subconscious. All the while we wear the loyalty to our family like a badge on our sleeve and continue to display it proudly in our everyday existence. We may, within the context of this life, dream of one day, many, many years from now, when it might be safe to look at all of this differently — but not now, not today. For what would be the results if we did? Who would feed and clothe us, take us to school, and give us the occasional feeling that we, in fact, do matter?

For many, this "aloneness" afflicts us so profoundly that we learn at a young age the very sophisticated process of *splitting*. We learn to take our true essence and compartmentalize it away — afraid it could endanger our existence within the tribe. If we were lucky, we may have found ways to take our true self out on occasion and dance with it. Ultimately, the sweet fruit that is found between these two split worlds is the substance that calls us to our adolescent journey. By recognizing that we are splitting, normally at the age of thirteen, we are called to begin the dance with our real self and begin at first a separation of and ultimately an integration of these two selves. When this passage is not successfully mastered, we find other ways to keep the real self alive — even if it is on life support. We may even find ways to do this through unhealthy means — means that may involve tools such as drugs or alcohol that help us mute or silence the family voices and allow us to have a moment *alone* with ourselves.

Where the like have classically been tagged as agents for numbing of the *self*, they sometimes serve as numbing agents not for ourselves but for the world around us, for those elements that prevent us from having a union with ourselves. But these numbing agents take a toll on us by *stopping the clock*. There are many ways in which the lost and lonely childhood soul, like the prodigal son, tries to find its way home, and blessed with a natural drive not to stop in this pursuit, he or she finds ways to continue the meetings with the truer self, even if in secret.

Ultimately we know that finding true peace within ourselves and our family involves a reunion with our true selves. This is not a small task, and for many, it comes to us involuntarily or even

14

spontaneously — *a calling*, as it were, on our own journey. It is often this act, or this rebirthing of *ourselves*, that leads us to a new state of being and a longing to crack through the wall of the deeply seated false self that was fostered with the willing participation of our family.

Such a calling may reveal itself to us as an involuntary moment in less than desirable circumstances — a moment that may require us to completely pull away from our family and its story. When that moment comes, we stand alone with ourselves and may have to endure a period of deep turbulence, as the prodigal son found himself alone with the pigs at the trough. It is only by passing *through* this separation that we can begin to experience our tribe or family of origin differently.

As the prodigal son showed us, the journey may begin with an unrecognized hardship. We must recognize that, like him, we must answer the call and take *the first step* on our journey, however lonely and awkward it may initially feel. It is this step that will ultimately lead us home.

Discovering Ourselves through Love

All these things shall love do unto you that you may know the secrets of your heart, and in that knowledge become a fragment of Life's heart.

- Kahlil Gibran, *The Prophet*

One of the fastest ways that we can shed the false self and find a path back to our true essence may be through the simple act of falling in love. When we find one other soul on the planet who can see into our true essence, it helps us find our way home to a lost self that may have remained unavailable to us for many years. This shift from being alone with ourselves to lifting the window shades and letting the light in can be very intoxicating. As we for the first time experience ourselves as never before, seeing into our own soul through another's eyes, we find our hearts warmed by the light of the knowledge that we were not meant to be alone. Someone else now bears witness to our true self.

For me, this experience came on quickly when Rich and I met. Our meeting, courtship, and eventual creation of our own family were all accomplished in lightning speed. We both had felt a need to rebuild the circles of our lives and families. There was an underlying panic to our meeting and courtship, one that pushed us both into the passing lane, unable to turn back in ways we could not even begin to understand at the time. I cannot explain what this urgency was about except to say that upon meeting we sparked something in each other – something that reminded each of us of our unrecognized potential and of the time that we had both lost up until this moment.

In the face of this unspoken urgency, Rich and I met, became engaged, and married within seven months. I remember standing at our wedding, knowing that neither of our families had had time to digest what was happening — the merger of two very different family stories and cultures. There were moments that first year when members of our families would act like referees at a football game, throwing yellow flags onto the field to remind us when we were veering too from the predictable family patterns. Everyone had words of advice, and ultimately it was Rich's father who cast the prediction that the new relationship and future marriage was bound for early failure. Imagine entering into your own family, your new union, with such a curse cast on you from your own tribe.

In those early years of our life together, we would often operate from a defensive and reactive place when it came to finding our new family culture with each other and how we would interact with our respective families. And although we had the initial blessing of finding one another and rediscovering our lost selves, we were each in many respects thrust back into the defensiveness of our false and adolescent selves until years later when we were able find the space to separate ourselves and to recognize and alter the way we saw ourselves in relation to our family stories.

Building New Circles

When an individual is raised in a family in which the nurturing circles of life and family have been choked by the stresses of life, and parents have not had a chance to grow into their own adulthood, there can be great resistance to the child's marriage or partnership and entry into adulthood and the outside world.

The tension between the newly discovered lost child and the parents' or family's strong resistance to this discovery can cause great turbulence in family relations, often masking itself as a lack of acceptance by the family. What is often misunderstood in this moment, however, is that this lack of acceptance represents a resistance of *the family of origin* to time marching on — to letting the circles of life take their natural and progressive next stages of growth — not necessarily to the introduction of the new family member.

This resistance may also be masked by other concerns, acted out far into the later years of the marriage as the adult child and his or her new spouse try to reconcile the new family with the old, all the while feeling very confused about why the union has become so difficult.

Creating a new family within a larger family that has not had the space, love, and resources to grow in a healthy, balanced, and natural way can be challenging. Ultimately, the mere idea that the grown child is creating a new branch in the family tree before the parents are ready to accept such an event leaves the entire family tree in a state of shock and sometimes even desperation — setting up the

17

next generation for yet another cycle of imbalance and family challenges. This passage and ritual, which would normally be viewed as something to be cherished and celebrated, may instead be viewed as an unwelcome and threatening event.

I can completely understand a parent's pain and sadness at watching his or her children grow, even when the children act in the spirit of finding their own way. I believe that my own parents, like the prodigal father, would have preferred to hold on to me a bit longer as *their daughter* before I took on the roles of wife and mother.

Husbands and Wives

Nobody's ready for marriage – marriage makes you ready for marriage.

- David Schnarch, *The Passionate Marriage*

After nearly sixteen years of marriage, it has begun to sink in that what goes on between Rich and me is a world that no one else will ever know. I do not mean that I am consciously keeping the interactions of our marriage private, but that the colors and texture of a relationship that for so many years carries so many functions and responsibilities develops a deepness in its character that is unmatched by any other relationship in our lives.

I can remember the nervousness I felt as Rich and I crossed the threshold of our thirteenth wedding anniversary, acutely aware that my own parents had parted ways during that year and that my father and his second wife had also called it quits right about this time. But what is interesting to me now is how irrelevant that was to our relationship, yet how quickly we apply such expectations to our relationships.

When we allow patterns and events from our family's past to become relevant to who we are today, when we take on the events of our parents' marriage — a very private and intimate affair between two people —we run the risk of applying expectations to our own marriage that have nothing to do with who we are or where we are going.

Misinterpretation of patterns is the essence of the story of Oedipus. Like so many of us, Oedipus's parents were proactive in doing what they thought was the right thing to avoid tragedy based on the prophecy they were given about their newborn son. In their quickness to act, they instead set up the circumstances through which the prophecy was unavoidable.

The spousal or partnership relationship must maintain a delicate balance of honoring the family forces from which each person came while simultaneously understanding that the marriage or union is the unique blending of two souls and their life together on a day-to-day basis. What we take from our families must be examined in the marriage more than in any other place.

19

What is so interesting to remember about marriage, on the other hand, is the understanding that every interaction that takes place between a husband and wife in the presence of their children can become the cultural gospel of the family. In every conversation Rich and I have, we are not alone. Even if our children are not present for a particular discussion, the implications of that discussion, what decisions are made, and how we treat one another in the context of the conversation affect how our children treat each other, anyone else they interact with, and ultimately themselves.

Husbands and wives hold a special place in the family lineage. Marriage is the only family relationship in which a choice of partner is made, and therefore it carries with it a special set of burdens and responsibilities.

In his book, the *Passionate Marriage*, David Schnarch talks about how many of the couples he has counseled were married for less than altruistic reasons, sometimes out of a fear of being alone or a need to be taken care of. Once together, regardless of the circumstances that brought them together, all couples must work together, learning to respect the separateness of each other while learning to find harmony in their togetherness.

It is the intensity and closeness of marriage as it sits at the top of the family relationship pyramid that makes it even more pronounced in its potential to create both pain and love within the relationship and the family as a whole. We can be having a joyous moment; then a misunderstanding can transpire and everything can shift from harmony and love to resentment and hurt in an instant. When this happens, it is not unusual for us to berate not only our partner, but ourselves, for having made the choices that have brought us here to this place. We begin to question and criticize, as well, our inability to *be better at managing the relationship.*

Realistically, however, we must come to terms with the fact that managing our relationship implies that we must manage the other *person* in the relationship. But if we believe that we cannot exist in a state of love and a state of fear in the same moment, we must also acknowledge that we cannot manage another person, *even in marriage.* When we begin to feel that we are somehow in charge of controlling our partner, that *we have some clue about how they are supposed to evolve* and that *we are somehow in charge of this*, we begin down a very slippery slope that leads us into a place outside of reality.

One interaction transpires in our family again and again. Rich comes home from a day's work, tired and with little energy for family life, and reverts to what I refer to as his "sarcastic self." He makes sarcastic jokes with the children, but often he is trying to gain their attention and illustrate a point that he feels otherwise would be lost on deaf ears. When hearing his sarcastic comments, I begin to criticize him directly and openly in front of the children. He usually reminds me that, although not perfect, he does have a point that he is trying to communicate. He will also remind me that it is important for him to have his own relationship with our children and that I am, in fact, undermining my children's intelligence by not letting them have their own interaction with him.

When I can step back from this conversation and hear his feedback as an adult and not as a wounded child, I am able to appreciate what Rich is saying. When I am trapped inside my own fear and my inability to trust Rich and the kids to evolve their own relationship, it becomes virtually impossible for me to step back and have faith in the outcome of their interaction.

In the example I have shared, Rich and the children and I are entering into something Murray Bowen, one of the founders of family systems therapy, refers to this as the "triangle." In his metaphor as outlined by *The Bowen Center for the Study of the Family*, Bowen describes the triangle as "a three-person relationship system. It is considered the building block or 'molecule' of larger emotional systems because a triangle is the smallest stable relationship system." Bowen argues that, "A two-person system is unstable because it tolerates little tension before involving a third person. A triangle can contain much more tension without involving another person because the tension can shift around three relationships. If the tension is too high for one triangle to contain, it spreads to a series of 'interlocking' triangles."

By interjecting myself into the interaction between Rich and our kids, I am showing my *own* distrust in the relationship between Rich and each of our children. When I do this, I am no longer in a state of *love*, but rather in a state of fear. My effort to control Rich's interactions are based on my *fear* that his sarcasm will grow out of control, that my kids will not be able to handle it, and that the entire system of communications in our family will eventually be broken down. It is this fear and the act of trying to control our partners that is so toxic to the institution of marriage and all family relationships.

The truth of the matter, when I am calm enough look at it, is more like this: Rich is tired and under stress and wants to limit the amount of negotiating he has to do with his kids. The kids understand how Daddy is acting and usually will let him know their feelings about this with their own words. Daddy gets a good night's sleep and most often has a reconstructive conversation with the kids the next day about whatever was frustrating him the day before.

The more I interject myself in Rich's relationship with our kids and create a *triangle* within their relationship, the more I complicate the situation. In 1915, Polish mathematician Wacław Sierpiński developed something that has since been referred to as *Sierpinski's Triangle* (shown in Figure 1). The triangle beautifully illustrates family triangulation (as described by Murray Bowen) with an added dimension. In the shape of the triangle, Sierpinski illustrates that if you create a geometrical set of triangles *within* the triangle, an infinite set of triangles can be built. The inner triangles are created again and again using something called *fractal replication*. A *fractal* is defined by Wikipedia as "a rough or fragmented geometric shape that can be split into parts, each of which is (at least approximately) a reduced-size copy of the whole." The joining of Bowen's theory of triangles in relationships along with Sierpinski's model of the infinite replication of triangles inside one another provide a wonderful image of what happens when we keep engaging in triangulation within relationships. Marriage is a classic container for just such behavior.

Figure 1. Sierpinski's Triangle

When we try to facilitate communications or harmony in another person's relationships, we risk, like the interlocking triangles, creating more complications and even bigger breakdowns in communications. The two other parties involved do not have a chance to clear the space and communicate directly. When I step out of the situation with Rich and any one of our kids, they keep trying and eventually find their own resolution. Usually a great lesson unfolds as they continue to perfect the art of communication with one another in an imperfect world and situation.

The moment we *objectify* our partner is the moment when we are no longer "in relation" with that person. The minute we step inside the relationships of our spouses and our children, we are objectifying each of them — working from a place of control which ultimately has its roots in fear, not love. Many couples underestimate the importance of remaining in relation to one another in a marriage and the divisiveness of interfering with each other's parent-child relationships.

Additionally, many of us enter into marriage with preconceived ideas of how marriage should work, what it should look like, and what function it should serve. Marriage, as Schnarch points out, is something no one comes prepared for. Even if we are marrying a second time, we cannot prepare for the relationship with the new person based on our experiences with our prior spouse.

We can only enter into this relationship with an open heart and open mind and remember two important things: First, the person we are married to was not put on this planet to serve us. They may *give* to us, but we cannot come to expect that they have an exclusive mandate to serve our every need and expectation. Second, we cannot predict let alone control the direction in which our partner's life journey will take him or her.

This said, the challenge of marriage becomes twofold: First, we are called to maintain our sense of love and acceptance for one another while remembering and honoring the uniqueness of our relationship. Our relationship is *not* a replica of our parents' relationship. Second, we must continue vigilantly to create a space in which our partner can grow, develop, and explore his or her own talents and abilities and relationships with other members of the family. We must have faith and acknowledge that our partner's journey is vastly different from our own and respect the steps that they need to take without interference. We must also remember, as we enter into the parenting years, that our spouse is on his or her own journey and has his or her own unique relationship with our children.

In summary, it is the sacredness and uniqueness of marriage that must be continually honored, understanding that we cannot control the destiny of another, and the more we try, the more the path will become tangled and unmanageable. Like the prodigal father's ability to let his son go and embrace him upon his return, our marriage may require from us a level of relinquishment on a daily basis. As we learn to let our partner have his or her own higher power, own voice, and own interactions unedited with the world around them, we stand the greatest chance of building a strong family. Each relationship is honored and has a chance to blossom; the truth that we cannot control one another but can only love and cherish the time we have together becomes the reality of our family story.

Parents and Children

And he arose and came to his father.
But while he was still a long way off, his father saw him and felt compassion,
And ran and embraced him and kissed him.

The Prodigal Son - Luke 15:11–32

The relationship between a parent and a child is in many ways the most revered relationship in the culture of family. With a purity that goes beyond the romantic bond, the relationship between a parent and a child is the most sacrificial and deeply mystical of all of the family relationships. Parenting, more than any other relationship, carries with it a specific set of responsibilities and is the most "job-like" of all the relationships we have. As children, we are from the beginning indoctrinated with the belief that our parents are our role models — the people we look to and *up* to — the ones we can count on to teach us proper guidance and modeling and help us find our way forward into adulthood.

One of my favorite gifts as a small child was getting to watch my father reinvent himself. Although his work as an artist and gallery owner remained a constant during my early years, he pursued many other interests with equal fervor. I can remember when he decided after years of sailboat racing to build his own boat. He knew that he was going to have to spend many hours learning the necessary physics and mechanics that would be required to create the blueprints. He would stay up late into the night, sometimes until three or four in the morning, educating himself on boat design and building.

Although the act of building the boat took a large toll on our family, the time I spent watching my father develop a new part of himself was not lost to me. It was instilled at a young age that no matter how old we are, we are never too old to learn something new, no matter how big it is.

In Angeles Arienn's book, *The Four-Fold Way*, she outlines the importance of balancing the four principal archetypes of warrior, healer, visionary, and teacher. Traditionally, we think of parenting more than any of the other three as a teaching role. But ultimately,

25

parenting requires the same amount of balance as any other life activity as described in Arienn's work. When we can show our children that we are still warriors and that we have visions beyond our current life, we open pathways for *our children* inside themselves, making them aware of what is possible in life and within their own reality. We create a hard-coded truth that the perceived limits of life are not real and that the line is only there for us to step over. Of all of the experiences our children will have, the one we can almost guarantee is that they will face circumstances and tasks that will challenge who they are. And although we ideally enter into parenthood with some amount of maturity, when we can share with our children the details of how we faced and overcame our own challenges, it instills in them the same sense of faith and belief in what is possible.

Moving from our warrior and visionary roles as a parent, we must also continue with the challenging role of the teacher. Parenting requires large doses of "toeing the line." We must be firm, hold to our rules, remain consistent, and keep standards. This delicate balancing of remaining in a role of authority while simultaneously completely embracing your child on his or her own path can be tricky.

One of the processes Bowen identified in work on family systems particularly important to the parent-child relationship is the process of *projection*. Bowen describes how parents can find ways to annihilate the authentic self of their children through this simple yet powerful process. The process of projection occurs when a parent takes an internal character trait that he or she holds with great fear or anxiety and projects that fear or trait onto the child as a way for the parent to relieve his or her own anxiety.

Bowen's projection process includes the following three characteristics:

1. **The parent focuses on a child out of fear that something is wrong with the child.** Although this fear may appear to originate with the child's behavior, usually it manifests from something the parent has experienced in his or her own life — an unresolved episode of their own childhood or an issue they have struggled with for quite some time. It may involve lost dreams, unresolved conflicts, unrealized potential, or

weaknesses that the parent has fallen prey to in their own youth.

2. **The parent interprets the child's behavior as confirming the fear.** When a parent projects this fear onto a child, the child naturally begins to internalize this new role and identity. As Alice Miller discusses in her book, *The Gifted Child*, children will adapt to their parents' views as a means of survival — *even* if this means abandoning their own authentic selves in the process. The parent watches closely for clues that the child's behavior fits the mold of the story for years and confirms them at every opportunity. When the reward may not necessarily be positive, the child's behavior that is in fitting with the projected fear elicits a strong response nonetheless. The reinforced ritual continues to validate and strengthen the child's new false identity.

3. **The parent treats the child as if something is wrong with the child.** Finally, the child responds consistently enough of the time that the parent is able to legitimately validate his or her views. The child *has* become the person the parent feared he or she would become. And with an almost fatalistic sense of resolve, the parent may at this point give up on the child completely.

The projection paradigm presented by Bowen is sad and oftentimes proves to sow the first seeds of the journey of a prodigal son. A child is left with no choice but to leave the circle and abandon both family and the projected false self to seek out new lands and people who can help him or her recover the true and lost self once again.

In the separation and void left by the missing child, the parents are often left with nothing but the projected image. They are left alone with the words, the thoughts, the ideas that they had previously so conveniently pinned onto the child. There is an uncomfortable void — one in which the parents, if they are fortunate, may begin to revisit the root causes of the projection.

Upon my graduation from college I moved into a small apartment in Boston with little furniture. I had just started a job but had no way of coming up with the extra money needed to put together a kitchen and particularly to buy silverware. I sat in the car one day with my mother a few days before moving into my new place and asked if she would not mind giving or loaning me the money for the silverware. My mother recounted a story of her own youth, when she was in a similar position. It became clear to me that she was not comfortable buying me the silverware because of what it represented in her own story. She felt it was important that I have the same experiences she had had, and by simply purchasing the silverware for me, I may be missing an important experience and lesson. My mother's reaction is typical of parents who feel the need to project their own experiences onto their children. When we are able to have our own experiences that are different from those our parents had, even if it means a physical separation, we and our parents can experience a moment of enlightenment. When parents are left with nothing but a shadow where a child once stood onto whom the parents were previously able to project an image, they are left with nothing but their own shadow and a chance to maybe for the first time explore its meaning.

The "abandonment" of family or leaving of the prodigal child is a gift not just for the child, but also the parent or parents, who may for the first time be able to see the labels and projections they have possibly falsely place on their child for too long. The recognition of such projections can serve as a call for *both* the parent and child — one that when answered can provide a new individuation for all family members that raises each of them to a place of new respect and compassion for one another.

Ultimately, parents and children must sometimes lay down their roles and step back and look at one another as people. Any way that this can be done can be very healing. When we look at the reunion between the prodigal son and his father, we see glimpses of this. Although the primary relationship was that of father and son, the gift of the story is their ability to celebrate one another as two souls who could see each other with deep love and compassion. Every once and again a moment will present itself when we are left with the opportunity to break from the *job* of raising a child or the *role* of being raised as a child to acknowledge and honor one another for the gifts we have brought into to one another's lives.

When we stop and recognize the humanness in each other, time almost stands still. The prodigal son found his own awakening

28

in his humility and his lost self, but the love and compassion that was offered by his father was a gift that allowed healing not only as for the son as an individual but in the family circle and generations to come.

Siblings

*But he was angry and refused to go in. His father came out and
entreated him,
But he answered his father, "Look, these many years I have served you,
And I never disobeyed your command, yet you never gave me a young
goat,
That I might celebrate with my friends. But when this son of yours came,
Who has devoured your property with prostitutes, you killed the fattened
calf for him!"*

- The Prodigal Son - Luke 15:11–32

There is no relationship that holds the potential for such gifts and
contains as much power as the sibling bond. Yet sibling relationships,
among all the family relationships, can often be the most
misunderstood, painful, and difficult to heal.

I have heard great stories of fathers and sons who have
reunited later in life, and I have even a seen a few marriages that have
been rebuilt from the ashes of divorce, but the sibling reconciliation
often requires much deeper levels of reflection, emotional
reorganization, and forgiveness to find its way home.

Why is the sibling bond so complicated and why does it carry
so much baggage? The answer lies partly in the fact that by its very
nature, *the sibling bond begins in the context of the triangle*. Siblings,
although connected to one another directly in their relationship, are
from the beginning part of a deeper relationship between them *and*
one or both of the parents.

As illustrated by the triangle model in Figure 1, most strained
relationships, I believe, have their roots in two individuals who are
unable to deal directly with one another and instead are party to
continuous interference between the two of them and a third entity
or person. I believe the primary cause of a strained sibling
relationship stems from the fact that conflicting siblings continue to
involve one or both parents in the sibling relationship, even if the
parents are no longer in the room, in their lives, or even alive. This
triangle between the siblings and the voice of the parent dictates the
nature of the sibling relationship, sometimes for their entire lives,
never allowing them to be free to get to know and enjoy each other

as individuals, separate from the ever-present voice of their parent's approval and judgment. The sibling bond becomes thick with the story of lost love and approval from the missing parent and is challenged to recreate itself as an honest connection between two people. Often it continues to exist as a living testament to an earlier passage in life — one where two people were left to only relate in a competitive way and not allowed to become who they might have in direct relationship to one another were they provided the proper love and respect.

One of my favorite stories of sibling relationships is the story of "The Three Little Pigs." The story, believed to data back to the late eighteenth century, presents the naïve, youthful, and enthusiastic effort of the three pigs to each build his own house. Most of the emphasis in our cultural interpretation of this story, however, has been on the wolf who was there to threaten each pig in his home. But at some point I started looking at these little pigs and the wolf very differently.

I began to see that there was a consensus among how most people saw the story: that the pigs were brothers, with each one using his own means and material to find his own way. Imagine for a moment that when the first pig loses his house made of hay to the wolf at the door, he is compelled to seek shelter at the second pig's house, made of sticks. Together the two pigs temporarily find safety until the wolf once again finds them and tears down their efforts. Then they find their way to the third pig's house, where joined in their forces, they trick the wolf and invite him down the chimney and cook him in the caldron.

The wolf ultimately represents the unconscious voices of the judgment of our parents, haunting us generation after generation. The pigs represent us as people in our relationships with our siblings, trying to find safety with one another away from the judgment of our parents — *the wolf as the voice*. The journeys we take individually and in our sibling relationships are often set up to fail by this invisible destructive force — a force that our parents most likely have not consciously burdened us with. Because of circumstances — which likely included inadequate amounts of attention and subtle and continuous inferences that caused us to remain in a constant state of competition with our siblings — many of us have become like the pigs, running from house to house, only to get taken down again by the spirit of our parents' early yet lingering criticism.

31

Ultimately, however, the story illustrates the power of what can happen when siblings band together in their effort to disable the forces of the wolf at the door. My English teacher in high school, who provided powerful role modeling in my life during my impressionable adolescent years, had three young children who are now grown. She has since shared with me a beautiful story about her and her husband still paying the cell phone bills for their three children — all of them out of college or in graduate school. What she (and I) found so deeply touching is that when she would get the cell phone bills, she would notice that most of calls her kids were making were not to their friends or even to their parents but to each other. As a parent, there are few greater gifts than knowing we have raised our children to be friends with one another.

In addition to the pigs-as-brothers analogy, the pigs in the story can also represent each of us moving through our own stages of life. The first pig's story represents our journey through adolescence, with our first attempt at creating a structure that is uniquely our own — but without the strength necessary to maintain this newfound identity in the face of the wolf at the door. With a house made of straw, the wolf as the voice of parental judgment easily finds us and takes us down. We are easily exposed, and our thin veil of self-confidence is quickly dismantled. Our true self, of course, is still intact, but our first attempt at exposing it is easily destroyed.

On the journey into later life, the second pig represents our more seasoned and even experienced self, still facing the wolf of our past generations, but this time with a more developed sense of self. The second pig may have even learned to master self-expression, build a more stable home, have a better sense of who he or she is, and may even be able to express this accordingly with a more sophisticated and stable house design. Ultimately, the *taking down* of the house of the second pig is no more difficult for the wolf. The second pig probably had more disappointment at the destruction of his house; he probably had worked harder building it and thought he had a stable solution.

Finally, there is the third pig. Life has provided him ample experience and stability of self-expression and he is able to construct a house that accurately reflects his deep and now developed and stable sense of self. Like the returning hero, the third pig is able to bring home the gift of his freedom of expression and share it with his other two brothers, bringing all of them onto equal footing. The wolf is no match for this pig and his stable home. The pig has *found* his home, and the wolf cannot take it from him.

I often think of parenting as winding up a small music box. When you are raising children, you spend years and years winding them up, feeding them with guidance, nurturing, and love. In the end you are left to release the crank and wait patiently to hear the song that they sing when they are released into the world. Their songs are their own; we cannot write them. We can only give them the nurturing, love, and shelter to build themselves up and leave and enter the world — to sing their own song. We hope that they are raised with enough sense of individuality, without living too much under the shadow of one another, that they become great allies to one another in later life.

As grown siblings, understanding our relationships with our brothers and sisters can provide us great awareness when we raise our own children. The first question to ask when trying to understand your relationship with your sibling is what parental voice is a continual presence in your relationship.

In watching my husband interact with his own grown brothers, I am reminded of the legacy his father has left with each of them— a legacy that has unfortunately undermined their ability to have loving and supportive relationships with one another. Having come to this country at a young age and worked hard to create a successful career in the American corporate world, Rich's father's path was one of great sacrifice and hard work. He was ripped early from his own culture, only to be thrust right away into raising a large family that included four boys. As a result of this, I believe Rich and possibly some of his other siblings were left with the message that they would each need to make it for themselves — without the support of each other — as their father had done.

Instilling our children with a sense of caring and concern for one another is ultimately one of the greatest challenges of parenting siblings. The more siblings there are, the more complicated the interlocking triangles of competition can become, and the more we are challenged with untangling these triangles to find a clear and honest relationship with one another.

No more does this message echo than in the story of the prodigal son. Despite the humble return of the son, there is no reconciliation between the two brothers. While the father and the returning son are able to find their way to a new union, the story leaves us with the two

33

brothers still not connecting, and the brother who stayed still resentful and confused about the status of his returned brother, after all he had done wrong. That the story leaves so much about the sibling bond unanswered speaks volumes to the importance, mystery, and complexity of the sibling relationship. What would happen when the father has passed away? How would the two brothers find a communion with one another?

The power of the healed sibling relationship cannot be underestimated in its impact on future generations. When it is left unrealized, the impact can also be equally powerful. Children of feuding siblings will look longingly at their uncles and aunts and find sadness in not having access to these other family members. These relationships might have provided the children with a deeper understanding of themselves than they would be able to experience with their parents alone. They may also be burdened with the unconscious fear that their own sibling relationships might turn out like this, the only model they have.

In later life, our ability to devote love and energy into healing our sibling relationships can be deeply rewarding. If we are able to find some common ground with even one of our siblings in later life, the rewards of this reconciliation will be felt not only in our relationship with one another but throughout the entire family tree. When we are able to find a new way to relate to our siblings, when we are willing to hear, honor, and rise beyond the third voice in the room and ask, "Mother, Father, Are you still in the room?" we may be able to sit for the first time with our siblings and get to know one another in a new way. Possibly we may even discover our siblings for who they really are for the first time.

As we begin to explore the five circles of family development in the next chapter, we will see the effects that our family history has on us as we become adults and how not only our sibling relationships, but all of the relationships in our family hold new possibilities through our ability to make a deeper commitment to forgiveness and humility.

2. The Family Tree and the Five Circles

You are the bows from which your children as living arrows are sent forth.
The archer sees the mark upon the path of the infinite, and He bends you with
His might that His arrows may go swift and far.
Let your bending in the archer's hand be for gladness;
For even as he loves the arrow that flies, so He loves also the bow that is stable.
- Kahlil Gibran, *The Prophet*

Like all other organic cooperative systems in nature, families are delicate ecosystems. As a family grows, it requires a certain amount of togetherness, separateness, and nurturing to become healthy and whole. When parts of an ecosystem are out of balance, the entire system can become out of balance.

A more specific analogy of family structure as represented in nature is that of the rings that grow inside the trunk of a tree. In the family, like the tree, each ring represents a new generation and even a new member of the family. *Dendrochronology,* or the study of tree-ring dating, states that each ring on a tree represents roughly a year in the tree's life. When a season has been particularly difficult, the rings appear thinner and less healthy. When the tree has had adequate nurturing, water, and sunlight, the rings are wider.

Considering that a family grows and matures like a tree, with its rings growing stronger and more robust with proper nutrients, we can imagine how years of poverty and depression can affect the growth of a family. In a family where there is balance among its individuals' needs for nurturing, there is room for each person to grow in an appropriate way. When nurturing is compromised, be it through divorce, illness, or financial difficulty, the growth of the family members may become stunted.

The Circles in My Own Family Tree

Because I was given a great deal of personal freedom as a child, I was able to let my own creativity develop at an early age. After my mother left when I was seven, my father carried the jobs of running his business, being an artist, and the primary parent raising four children. Ironically, my father had also somewhat raised himself as a young person and, like me, had developed the ability to take on a lot of responsibility. There was nothing he thought he could not do, and the mere thought of not being able to accomplish something he felt was important to him would make him uneasy.

There was another side, however, to my father's ability to take everything on – especially when it came to raising children. I can remember childhood years when my brothers, sister, and I were left alone many of the evening hours while my father worked. The "rings" of the tree, so to speak, during these years were skinny and very close together. The atmosphere in our house was one of "Every man, woman, and child ... okay, every child...for himself!" The four of us were often left in charge of ourselves and of the house, keeping it clean, preparing dinner, and in general running the ship.

These years left me with a deep sense of how important guidance is in a child's life. As I have gotten older and particularly into my forties, I am still amazed how small redirections from others can help us refocus ourselves back on course at times when we are otherwise paralyzed with indecision. During these early years I knew I had a capable mind, but I had little sense of how to use it. Schoolwork seemed strange to me as I did not have a clear sense of why it was given to me or what the value was in completing it. I would take it on with a detached effort – as if I were throwing darts at the dart board, with no clue if what I was doing would actually make the bull's eye. Being left on my own a great deal of the time left me with deficits in my ability to foster consistency and discipline in my learning efforts which I believe ultimately kept me from achieving some of the things I was capable of in life sooner.

My husband, on the other hand, grew up on an entirely different type of ship which in turn contributed to his ability to maintain such discipline and an ability to finish things that I am still trying to master. With ten people living under one roof and a mother

36

who tightly managed the entire operation, as chaotic and crazy as it sometimes became, there was for Rich always a sense of belonging. Each person operated as a part of the whole, and although he certainly had less time and space to be alone and find his inner creative voice, he was able to function as part of a team, coexist with many other personalities, and successfully contribute to the overall maintenance of the household, ultimately giving him the confidence to know he could get things done.

Although much later in our marriage we were both gifted with the insight of our different family cultures, it would be years before we could appreciate this. When Rich and I were expecting our first child and starting our own family, we began to unravel these truths, but not all at once. In these early years, we were instead left with the naked truth that *neither of us had had adequate time to get grounded in who we were as grownups prior to starting our own family.* It was most likely a subconscious knowing of this that begged us to find a fresh ground on which we could have a new family beginning.

Conflicted with the fact that we knew our children would benefit from contact with relatives and specifically grandparents, we decided before the birth of our first son to move away and find a neutral ground where we could begin our lives as a family. Although we knew in our hearts that this was the right decision, it was hard to silence the internal voices that begged us to stay put. As Angeles Arienn states, we have only two choices in life: we can either continue a pattern we know or we can transform it. We knew that if we were to stay on the east coast and raise our family, the possibility of changing family patterns would be limited by our loyalty to the codes we already knew. In other words, we knew that we needed to find the courage and energy to move beyond these old circles – both physically and emotionally – to create our own rings in the tree.

The Five Circles

After our move to California, I began to look at my role within my family of origin and take inventory. I classified different areas of life into "circles" that sat symbolically one inside the other. Like the rings that grow in the trunk of the tree, these circles and their relationship with one another represented to me the patterns of growth in my own life's journey – the times when I was able to move forward and mature as well as the times when there was little to nurture me, when all I could do was maintain my skinny self in the presence of the chaos around me.

As I began to see my life in the framework of the circles of the tree, I began to give names to these circles and identify those – five in total – that I believe represent the components that make up our life within the family structure.

The First Circle represents our true essence — the self we are born with as our natural set of gifts. This circle is the place where the self we are born with lives. There is no judgment in this place, no self-criticism or shame. There is only self-love. When we are still, we are easily reunited with our true essence.

When our first circle has the proper room to grow, we experience a life of harmony in which our true talents and gifts are both realized and practiced day to day.

The Second Circle is the layer that both protects us from and enables us to connect with the outside world. When the second circle becomes too thick, we have trouble making a connection between our true self and the outside world. A symptom of a thick second circle is the overdeveloped ego, in which every interaction we have becomes more about ourselves and our sense of confidence than anything or anyone else we interact with.

The Third Circle represents our life within our family – the people we live with on a day-to-day basis and break bread with. The life in the third circle is the life of a growing family, the dinner table, children, and the growth of a new generation. A third circle out of balance may involve childhood neglect or deprivation of vital resources. It may cause us to repeat old patterns of faulty code that have been handed down to us, despite our best intentions and wishes to do otherwise.

The Fourth Circle is our life beyond ourselves and our family. Our fourth circle becomes the border at which our family life meets the edge of culture, our work or livelihood, community, and the place where we live. When our first three inner circles are out of balance, our interactions with the fourth circle may become inappropriate, exaggerated, or strained. In other words, because we cannot function comfortably within ourselves or our family, the outside world may become a haven of escape from these inner circles.

The Fifth Circle is realized when we are able to surrender and find balance and allow our life energy to flow freely throughout the other four circles in our life – creating the ultimate sense of wholeness. When we have discovered our fifth circle, we will know it because we will recognize that our energy is moving freely through all areas of our life. When our other four circles are out of balance or feel blocked or disconnected from one another, our fifth circle will be nearly impossible to see. When we can find our fifth circle, the thoughts, people, and passages that once seemed impossible to integrate into our life may begin to feel connected and we feel full of hope and love.

Figure two illustrates the five circles and how they sit like the rings of a tree one inside the other and how they relate to different aspects of our life.

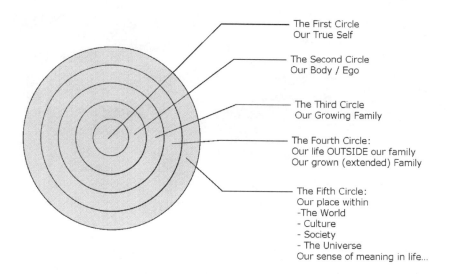

The First Circle
Our True Self

The Second Circle
Our Body / Ego

The Third Circle
Our Growing Family

The Fourth Circle:
Our life OUTSIDE our family
Our grown (extended) Family

The Fifth Circle:
Our place within
-The World
- Culture
- Society
- The Universe
Our sense of meaning in life...

Figure 2. The Five Circles

39

The First Circle

The fire of creativity is the fire that takes no wood.
- Angeles Arienn

It is our first circle that represents our true self or *spirit,* if you will, the part of us who may have for some time been lost or trapped deep inside us. This part of us, when recognized and in a state of balance, reverberates out into all the other circles of our life. It provides us with life energy and creates much of our reality. It is no wonder, then, that when we lose touch with our core self, we also lose touch with our life energy, becoming depressed, paralyzed, and exhausted in our efforts at living.

While many of us may maintain that this private and intimate part of ourselves is *separate* from the other aspects of our life, it is my belief that it is the integrity or *integration* of this core self with the other aspects of our life that ultimately heals our lives, our family, and the communities and world in which we live. It is our sophisticated and dysfunctional ability to live fractured lives that greatly contributes to our own sense of being disconnected in the world. As we continue daily to convince ourselves that we can block some of the circles from interacting with each other, we perpetuate our own discontent. Unfortunately, our mind's ability to compartmentalize in this way has allowed us to maintain such a way of life for centuries.

One of the ways we know that we are out of balance and out of touch with our first circle is that we are not really feeling things in our body and in our heart. We know this when we experience something profound or meaningful and instead of feeling an appropriate response of sadness or joy, we feel only anxiety or fear. Fear, I believe, when it is felt a great deal of the time (and especially when we are not in life-threatening situations), serves as a reminder that we have lost touch with our true self. When we are in a *state of fear,* our subconscious is telling us that we are at odds with ourselves. This constant state of fear, I argue, is more a fear of the truth that we are not living, not experiencing our true self, than a fear of anything else, even death.

Recently I was in church with my family and my oldest son, David, was altar serving, standing and holding a large candle next to the priest, who was finishing the gospel reading before beginning the homily. As the priest turned to walk to the center of the landing, he noticed that David was not following him but had sunk into a deep unresponsive trance and was not moving. The priest turned quickly to catch him and hold him up before he fell; David had become dizzy and unresponsive. At his usual Scotty-beam-me-up speed, Rich was gone from his seat next to me and at David's side at the front of the church before I even knew what had happened. I made my own dash for the two of them and, like Rich and Father Mike, began repeating David's name again and again, only to be met with a blank locked-in stare and a body about to collapse. Rich whisked him outside and laid him down on the grass, and he eventually began responding to us. In that moment, however, of seeing his still and vacant expression, I had the thought that I had lost him. Although there were the practical thoughts of what to do spinning through my mind, in those few seconds my heart sent only one single resounding message – how much I loved David and how much I would miss even our sharp-tongued bickering if I were to lose him. All at once I felt my truest self and its deepest expression: that of a mother who deeply loves her awkward thirteen-year-old son. There was no feeling bigger than that, no truer self than that, and all it took was one moment looking into the abyss of my own self to be reminded.

It sometimes takes such moments of reality, when life strips us of all of our pretenses, to remind us of who we are and what matters and ultimately call out the feelings of love that come shining through. As a good friend of mine recently pointed out when recounting the story of her husband's stroke, it is too bad that it is so hard to hold onto these feelings we are gifted with when we are close to the edge – moments that take us back to the place inside ourselves where everything matters, everything is real, and nothing can shake us.

Some of us, like the prodigal son, may have to go to great lengths to be reunited with our abandoned first circle. We must let our journey take us far away from all that we have been raised with in our own childhoods so that we may strip back the false layers and allow for the reunion with our truest self. We must remember that our true self is never gone from us; it is only in hiding. Like the sun behind clouds, we need only to find a sunny moment to reunite with it.

Some of the tools I have found helpful for remaining in this state of union are photographs of my truest moments in life. I keep them prominently featured in places in our home where I pass them daily. I also keep a large wicker box letters I have received over the course of my life from people I love. Sometimes all it takes to once again experience my authentic self is rereading a letter or two from a dear friend and remembering all the lives I have been touched by.

The Second Circle

He who tries to shine dims his own light

- Lao Tzu

Moving out beyond the first circle is the second circle. The second circle represents our *physical body as well as our ego* and serves as both a protective layer to the true self as well as a place where we hold all of the physical and psychological stories of our life.

As David Berceli discusses in his book, *The Revolutionary Trauma Release Process*, the physical body is the honest telling of our psychological and emotional story. During trauma, the events and stories of the moment are absorbed into a particular set of muscles in our body. The natural animal response to such an experience is to allow the body to enter into a deep state of shaking until the energy absorbed from such an event is released. When this process cannot be completed, the trauma stays lodged in our body and particularly muscles in our body's core that surround our vital organs, where it can remain dormant for years, thus increasing the power and imbalance in our second circle. Berceli's work helps us understand why we are in the place we are in and why we stay stuck in our relationships with family members. Additionally, it helps to explain why as families we are prone to retraumatize each other over and over in a sometimes escalating way.

This understanding of our body and its relationship to the physical and emotional events it undergoes in such circumstances is the key to understanding the role it plays in the second circle. While our mind may be highly skilled at reorganizing, retelling, and even denying the truth as a matter of survival, the body cannot lie. The body will carry this burden, suffer its ill effects, and even exhibit chronic pain or illness from trauma as a result of keeping the truth under wraps for so long.

The second circle teaches us that our relationship with our bodies and how well we listen to them directly affects our ability to relate and interact with both our inner self (the first circle) and the continuing outer circles (our families, friends, and community).

We cannot escape or underestimate the role our body plays in our relationships with ourselves, our families, and beyond. When we find ways to expel some of the energy that has accumulated in our body, especially around trauma and disappointment with our family, we can begin to clear space for new and more healthy ways to let our true and genuine energy move throughout our life.

In Ayurvedic medicine (the system of traditional medicine native to India), it is believed that all disease in our bodies originates as a temporary irritation; without proper treatment and left for long periods of time, such illnesses can result in an irreversible chronic condition. When we look at how we use our bodies as staging grounds to deal with the unprocessed issues in our lives, it is not such a mystery why the second circle, or the part of our lives that represents our ego and physical body, can become so out of balance with the rest of our lives.

I have spent a good deal of my life plagued with acne. Ultimately, I know that I have played a large part in the perpetuation of this condition in my body, as I am certain it has served a very important function in my life. Besides the symbolism of the acne as a reminder that I have not yet fully processed my own adolescence, it serves as a barrier between me (my first circle) and the outside world.

When my face breaks out (and when I perpetuate the problem by then picking at it), my interactions with the outside world are minimized. It may well be that in these moments I have so deeply lost touch with my true and inner self that the mere thought of interacting with the outside world feels far too threatening. Or it may simply be that I have temporarily lost my ability to maintain a healthy balance among all of the circles, and the broken-out face serves as the message that I must retreat until I can better balance these circles.

I have known many other people whose bodies have found similar mechanisms of retreat — skin ailments, bad stomachs, migraine headaches. Each of these physical issues serves to remind us of one simple fact: When we are out of balance, we are taking in from the outside more than we can process on the inside; eventually our body fights back and begins to protest the interactions going on around us.

Doctors tell us that the anecdotes for such ailments can be found in medicinal remedies — antibiotics to clear up our skin, antacids to calm our stomachs, or pain killers to relieve the pounding in our head. But if we are keeping our ear to the tracks, we know that there is a much more effective remedy to these issues, one that does not even require a trip to the doctor's office.

When our second circle is calling us and our body feels bigger or more burdened than it should, we can answer the call in two ways. First, we must look deep inside and ask ourselves what truth lies behind these triggers. What experiences has our body endured that are causing our face to break out, our stomach to hurt, or our brain to begin pounding? If we can gently ponder these as related to the issues of balance in our lives and our ability or inability to embrace and honor our true self, some of these ailments may fall away all on their own. Second, we can take on the ailments of our body by way of mothering ourselves. If we are overweight, we may want to make a commitment to once again honor our body and pay attention to what we are putting into it. If our face is continually breaking out, we may want to build a routine around taking care of it, even in small ways, so that we can begin to see small shifts in the balance of its PH levels.

These acts of caring for our body may be simple but will most likely be met with our deep resistance. The simple truth is that if we reduce the girth of our second circle and the buffer of our ego, we may be left to face the truth of how unintegrated the rest of the circles in our lives have become. It is important during these moments of truth that we are deeply patient and compassionate with ourselves in our understanding of what these barriers have provided for us over many, many years. There was a reason the prodigal son took his money and squandered it on reckless living. What else was he going to do to provoke an almost homeopathic reaction within himself? He did not know who he was anymore and had no appreciation for his family. It was all he could do to squander what he had in hopes of stirring something in his body. It was his only hope of restoring some semblance of balance within the circles of his life.

I have found Berceli's exercises particularly useful and try to recognize when I need to revisit them. There have been times when I have found my legs and lower body easily set into a state of shaking and I know that I am once again accumulating emotional debris into my second circle. By practicing these exercises along with other physical exercises such as running, yoga or just getting out for a walk, I am reminded of how I can guard against my second circle becoming too big and preventing me from sharing my true inner gifts with my family and the world around me.

The Third Circle

The Tao gives birth to One.
The One gives birth to Two.
The Two gives birth to Three.
The Three gives birth to all things.
- Lao Tzu

The third circle represents our life within our immediate family and the people we live with on a day-to-day basis. While we can choose our spouse, we cannot choose our parents or children. When we can entertain the idea that these people have been placed in our lives for a reason, we can begin to explore how we might be able to honor their true essence, and to, in a sense, *fall in love* with our families once again. We can find a level of respect and empathy not dissimilar to the feelings discovered for our spouse or partner when we first met.

One of the simplest ways to see whether our third circle is healthy and balanced is to listen to the voices of those we love and with whom we live. When our children are asking us repeatedly to hear their stories or when our spouse must tell us again and again that he or she is looking for us to help out around the house, it is a clear sign that we are not giving our third circle the proper amount of nurturing and attention that it needs.

Ironically, the third circle requires us to be a grown-up, and sometime event to put on the back burner our own hero's journey, our own adult continuation of our adolescent discovery in order to remember the young people pulling at our coat strings and asking not only for our approval but for our interaction and our attention. This can be hard and even painful at times when we are self-absorbed and busy trying to make sense of our own shattered childhood — and often the interactions we have with our children as they grow make us more and more aware of our own childhood passages.

I can remember a trip to Florida when my daughter Olivia had just turned four months old. It was a celebratory trip to visit my grandparents, to introduce them to their great grandchildren, and to celebrate thanksgiving with my brother, sister, mother, and Rich's oldest brother's family. There was so much at stake on this trip, so much crossing of so many circles that I believe the pressure caused

46

me to lose much of my focus on my own little family and my third circle. Working full time and with two small children, I had absorbed the social pressures of seeing myself as a less-than-perfect mother and insisted, even when traveling on the trip south, on making sure that I breast fed my daughter. I refused to acknowledge that, even prior to this long trip, my baby daughter had shown signs of being frustrated with my stoic breast-feeding regimen. She was often fussy when I would feed her and eventually became too upset to nurse except when I was standing up in a dark room. As we came closer to our long plane ride and trip across country to Florida, I became more and more stubborn in my position. After all, I was about to be reunited with my mother, grandmother, and sister, not to mention my sister-in-law who had children just a few years older than ours and who had served as a maternal role model for me. The last thing I wanted was to let down the breast-feeding-mom persona that I had so stoically preserved up until this point.

As it turned out, my daughter refused to nurse for nearly the entire trip to Florida. The stress that this miscalculation took on our entire family was big, and sadly, I spent a great deal of the trip completely obsessed with what my family was thinking about me and judging how good a job I was doing raising my own family. It was a typical example of how *as grown adults raising our own families, we can be completely preoccupied with our own ego, remaining in the role of our parents' child.* Looking back on this trip, I can imagine how my two-year-old son must have felt. There was so much focus on the adults, on recovering our balance from the rough start to the trip and to my concerns with trying to win my parents' approval that the entire point of the trip — that of giving my relatives a chance to bond with my kids — was completely lost.

While it is not hard to recognize when our third circle is out of balance, it is often hard to reset it. We may find ourselves with a young family and a deep need to speed the clock and hurry ourselves through the issues of our own adolescence, trying genuinely to become more responsible and make ourselves more available to our children.

One of the practical things we can do to remain true to our third circle is simply to keep the pulse on our own family's call to us. Our children are the best teachers we can have. They will do an amazing job of reminding us when we stray too far from our role as their parent. Our only challenge will be keeping our ear to the track and continuing the simple yet vigilant task of listening to them. Ultimately, the rite of passage of becoming a parent and loosening our grip on our own role as the child is one of the most delicate walks we must take. Our children do need us, and we must also remain true to ourselves and to our own journey if we are to serve as the role models that they need.

There are days when I know that I am not spending enough time with my family. I can recognize these moments from the fact that our house starts to feel messy and there has not been a sit down dinner in over a week. During these times, Rich and I try to do simple things like shut the shades, turn off all of the phones and watch a movie with the kids. It is important to just be together, even when life gets too hectic, as we need to remember how important it is to just be physically close and to enjoying each other's company.

The Fourth Circle

The soul walks not upon a line, neither does it grow like a reed.
The soul unfolds itself, like a lotus of countless petals.
                                        - Kahlil Gibran, *The Prophet*

The fourth circle represents all of our relationships with the world outside our home and our day-to-day existence with our self and our nuclear family. This circle includes our friends, work, hobbies, and for some, our extended family. The third and forth circles will often expand and contract in their relationship with one another in matters concerning the extended family. During times of transition, such as when we are first married or having our own children, these circles may shift in a turbulent and even destructive way, the way that the plates deep under the Earth shift during an earthquake.

When the third circle has been neglected in our own childhood, or when our parents have misused their power over us inappropriately when we were children, the experiences from those years may appear in later life and get acted or played out in our fourth circle. This circle is where much of the tension of growing up without a strong sense of self becomes evident. When we have not had a chance to adequately nurture the person we were meant to be, especially as it relates to our interaction with the outside world and our ability to have a livelihood that flows from our truest gifts, the conflicts of the fourth circle can be very painful.

For many years, I lived a very disingenuous existence within my own fourth circle. Landing in Boston after college, I took whatever random jobs I could find, eventually winding up at a large technology publishing company where my abilities to "fit in" and placate people were well utilized, but many of my truer and more powerful gifts went unrealized. My career, although dotted with moments of success, was made up of many unconscious choices. I fell prey to the circumstances of my random career choices, continually reacting and responding to the opportunities that were presented to me.

After my bout with breast cancer at forty-one, I began to understand that there was a deep, untapped set of gifts buried inside me, gifts that had never seen the light of day. When I began to recognize these gifts and talents, I began to see the great discrepancy between the things I had spent more than twenty years engaged in as a professional and my truest gifts. At first I used this awareness of the split in my life to berate myself. How could I have let myself fall so far away from what mattered to me? How had I become so passive in my efforts to build a career?

After spending a substantial amount of time beating myself up, a conversation with my editor reminded me of a simple but important truth. All those years I had spent in technology, learning to understand computers, write code, and analyze data were not in vain. The skills I had developed during these years had left me a great sense of how to look at life's nuances in ways that I might not have done otherwise. The mental muscles and sharp analytical skills I had developed certainly came in handy as I began to decipher the messages that were being downloaded to me at lightning speed during this transformative phase. I began to understand myself and my relationship with my family in a new way.

Ultimately I learned to embrace the duality I had found in myself while growing into my fourth circle. I found peace by example in the accomplishments and life story of Leonard Shlain, one of my favorite modern authors. Shlain is the author of the book *Goddess and the Alphabet,* which fundamentally defined our historical relationship with time, our right and left brain, and how these separate hemispheres of the brain defined the shifts between feminine and masculine energies that have dominated so much of our past century. In an interview before his passing in 2009, Shlain pointed out that although his life had taken him on a journey as an author that he might not have expected, which included a bout with cancer and a trip to the ancient ruins of Greece, he continued to maintain his life as the "father" of arthroscopic surgery and the head of the department at California Pacific Medical Center. Although he had discovered his new role as a writer and visionary, he also continued his work as a physician and surgeon.

Shlain's story and life work have served as a continual reminder to me that my path is unique and, although I may at times feel there are too many conflicting directions in life, this duality may be a necessary ingredient in my own journey. My life and my continual straddling of my two worlds – the world I have known as a wife, mother and technologist and my world as a student of our spiritual journey here on earth - must be honored if I am to discover a life that is more integrated. I cannot completely abandon the work I have known, however distant it may feel from the other calling that has found me.

When individuals are not permitted to grow into themselves in an appropriate manner, the tension of the conflicts that play out in our fourth circle can last for a long time. As a priest once told me, we can only change our lives from the place where we currently sit. From nowhere else is change possible.

In addition to our ability to find a livelihood that utilizes our truest gifts, our relationships with our friends and extended families are important aspects of the fourth circle. If we are raising a family, we will find a great deal of our time devoted to our third circle – to raising our own family. But we must still find time for the relatives who raised and came before us – our parents, grandparents, and aunts and uncles. We must learn to embrace these people and to find a place for them in the same way that we embrace our true self in our work and our ability to make a living.

The fourth circle is the place where we deliver our gifts to the world. It is the place where we honor our parents and relatives in the gifts they have given in raising us. The fourth circle is our bridge to the outside world, and if we can mange not to let it fall into too much disrepair, it can serve as the bridge that provides us *and our family* a safe passage into the outside world.

Often times I find the fourth circle to be the most difficult one to balance. As we become more aware of what this circle holds and how important it is to maintain integrity with how we work and interact with the outside world, it is not uncommon for stresses to arise around the pressure to re-craft our life in this circle too quickly. I always try to remember to keep in mind that no real change comes quickly and a house can only take so many changes to its foundation.

The Fifth Circle

The most precious gift we can offer others is our presence. When
mindfulness embraces those we love, they will bloom like flowers.
- Thich Nhat Hanh

The fifth circle represents our relationships with our community, culture, and world in which we live. It relates to and reconnects us with our other four circles – particularly our first circle. The fifth circle, if you will, represents the language and symbolism we have chosen to express our inner essence into the world and universe in which we exist.

The fifth circle includes our ethnicity, the type of community we live in (large city or small town), our philosophical and political beliefs, as well as our relationship to the planet as a whole. The other important component of the fifth circle is our ancestry. For those who still live in indigenous cultures (where cultural rituals, celebrations, and religious or spiritual beliefs are still intact, practiced, and supported by the surrounding communities and Earth), the fifth circle provides a strong outer membrane for our life and greatly contributes to our ability to build a balanced life within the other circles.

Our inner self (our first circle) is deeply connected to our fifth circle, especially when we have balance between the middle circles and ample space and time to reflect on the connection between the two. When, however, our second, third, and fourth circles are out of balance, it is likely that we will not even find our way to, let alone recognize, our fifth circle. The fifth circle represents our ability to find a complete connection between our inner self and the outer world. If we have not been able to connect completely with our truest self, the fifth circle will remain a mere dream to us. Our ability to find peace and see beyond our family and efforts to make a living will be extremely difficult.

I believe it is not possible to leapfrog over our middle circles and connect our first and fifth circles without first doing the practical work of being present in our lives and with our families. In other words, although there is an apparent connection between the innermost (self) and outermost (sense of meaning and peace in the world) circles, this union cannot be realized until we first make peace and find balance within the middle three circles.

My dear friend Cheryl once shared a wonderful parable with me. In the story, three men all found enlightenment. Upon this attainment, each of these men responded differently. The first went off and joined the monastery, where he happily continued his meditative practice and learned the discipline of peace and silence through this practice. The second man could not completely contain the profoundness of enlightenment and still exist in the earthly world, so he in fact went insane. The third man, however, simply returned home and kissed his wife.

Many of us experience a moment when we wake up from the dream of who we thought we were to find ourselves alone and naked with our authentic self in a life already built. At this moment, we must remember that our lives can only be recreated from the inside out; we must honor the life from which we came and ultimately take what we have learned and reintegrate it into our life.

For me, this truth revealed itself in the throes of finishing the final draft of this book. I had felt quite proud of myself to have finished the first pass, and I was a bit resistant my editor's final comments and integrating them back into the book. Although I knew there was nothing but truth and wisdom in the specific set of tasks he had left me with, the idea of once again returning to the solitary act of writing seemed more daunting than my previous writing efforts had been.

Ultimately the words of a friend set me free from this burden. I had expressed to Michelle some weeks back that I was struggling with how to join or mesh the two worlds in which I perceived I now lived – that of a new writer and self-appointed spiritualist and that of a wife and mother. One night while I was having dinner at her house, she took me aside and told me she remembered our earlier conversation and had been carrying it around ever since. Upon reflection, she said, she wanted me to understand one very important thing: As much as I longed to drift off with the books, talks, and intellectual gratification of my new spiritual endeavors, my real work was here on Earth as a wife and mother. I cannot express the comfort I found in her words. As she spoke, I felt something deep in my gut settle as it had never before and realized in that moment that for all my talents and accomplishments, for all the great and extraordinary things I had had the opportunity to be a part of, no one had ever given me permission to give my most sacred self to the raising and nurturing of my family.

     How ironic these words seemed as they settled into my body. Here I was running around touting myself as a sage of family experience, yet I could not find my own balance between raising my family and spreading my gospel. Ironically, Michelle's words left me free to finish editing the book, still able to focus on the fact that I could only do this as it served to maintain harmony within my own family.

As I grow into being a mother and a wife more and more each year, I feel blessed with the privilege of being part of my own new family history. I am also acutely aware that the moments I have to reflect on the blossoming of my true self sit alongside the time I get to spend as part of my own family. I am equally grateful when I can achieve a level of balance in my life among my marriage, my children, my work, and time spent simply being a child of God. When our first four circles find their proper balance, the fifth circle, the circle that allows us our deep and soulful expression of fitting into the bigger picture of life, can be fully embraced. Our fifth circle becomes visible to us once we provide the adequate time and nurturing required to our inner four circles. In the fifth circle is where all of our life has meaning and integrity and we can fall asleep each night at peace with how we lived our day.

Harmony within the Five Circles

If we have no peace, it is because we have forgotten that we belong to each other.

- Mother Teresa

In a healthy family, each member spends a balanced amount of time among the five circles. A healthy family, in other words, contains individuals who are able to maintain harmonious relationships with all of the five circles. When the circles become out of balance, we must consider three things.

First, maintaining a healthy relationship within our five circles requires us to maintain a well-differentiated sense of self. In other words, we must maintain an integrated sense of who we are as we exist in the world. When our true self is allowed to flow throughout all of the five circles in our life, we can belong to all of our circles in a harmonious way.

Second, each family member needs to remain healthy in his or her physical body. As Berceli discusses in *The Revolutionary Trauma Release Process*, when our bodies are out of balance or overcharged, the result can be dysfunctional behavior that wreaks havoc not only on our own health but also on the health of those we love. When we take care of our body, release its tension appropriately, and keep it in balance, we create a more harmonious and friendly environment for both ourselves and our family. By doing this, *we increase the possibility of balance in our lives, in our family's lives, and in the five circles.*

Lastly, much of the fracturing between family members comes when not enough attention is paid to the third circle and an unhealthy amount of attention is paid to the fourth circle. Typical examples of imbalance in these circles include individuals who spend too much of their time and energy nurturing their jobs, political interests, or hobbies while leaving little time and energy for the family. Even within the third circle, a delicate balance is required. Imbalances can be damaging over a long period of time, but they can be reset through conscious awareness of the circles and the importance of the attention and balance paid to each of them. When a family circle is restored after a significant period of imbalance, the relationships among the circle members are often stronger and more

55

meaningful and are treated with greater respect and appreciation than before.

The Earth itself provides a wonderful metaphor for us in understanding our relationship between our spirit (the core) and our physical bodies (the Earth). Chrystal Geysers, volcanic eruptions, and earthquakes are all ways in which the Earth releases her pressure. We, too, must find ways to release these pressures from our bodies, pressures that can be accumulated from years and years of stress, trauma, and mistreatment. If we continue to deny the messages of our body and do not find ways to release them, we are destined to stay trapped in our old ways of relating to one another through the history and language of our body. The circles of our life begin to feel more like prisons than reverberating exchanges of energy.

When the energy among all the circles and all the aspects of our life can flow freely, our true self can express itself and speak in the same way a stone sends circular waves when cast onto a still pond. While each of us in a balanced family represents just such a stone, the circular waves of the waves sent forth intersect, forming beautiful and intricate patterns, making up the wonderful and spontaneous moments of our relationships with the people we love. How well we are able both to experience and share our true self is ultimately dependent on how well we can honor and balance all of the circles in which we live.

As we explore these circles in our life, we may begin to see that there will be great changes ahead that can bring us immense joy, but as we approach these changes, we must also honor the transitions in all their stages. The chapters that follow provide us with some sign-posts we might recognize along the way on our road to forgiveness.

3. The Hero's Journey and Circles in Transition

We must let go of the life we have planned, so as to accept the one that is waiting for us.

        - Joseph Campbell, *Reflections on the Art of Living*

When we cannot experience our true selves in the presence of our family, childhood can be a very lonely passage in our lives. We can spend decades looking for an escape hatch — a way to release ourselves from our false existence, the one we diligently built to please those we loved during this chapter in our lives. Once we grow older and are able to recognize this false self for what it is and can see it in its opposition to our *true self*, we may finally have a chance to ask ourselves, "Is there a way back?"

Campbell and the Hero's Journey

There is a way back. The way back to our true self, however, demands three important things. It requires us to become the hero in our own family story. The hero's story, or *hero's journey* as it is called by Joseph Campbell in *The Power of Myth*, serves as a model for this book and has inspired me to understand my own life, as well as the parable of the prodigal son, in a new way.

What Campbell synthesized from years of studying the similarities among all major cultural mythological heroes was that each hero's journey fits a pattern. The pattern involves a process of *separation, transformation,* and *return.*

If we are to heal our relationships with ourselves and our family, we must take the same three steps. We may have to revisit them again and again as we find the courage to rewrite our family story.

1. **We must be open to passing through a phase of** *separation* **from our families for a period of time** — physically, emotionally, or both. In the hero's journey, this is called "answering the call." For many of us, this may be an instinctual call to a place or people or life away from the family we were raised with. We may feel uncomfortable and even guilty in this exodus, but its call may lead us somewhere we need to go but have yet to understand.

2. **We must be willing to undergo a** *transformation* — to be able to hear the truth of our family story in a new way and find forgiveness and release blame from all of those we have up until this point held accountable and responsible for our lives. This is the second phase of the hero's journey — also referred to as "the initiation." This phase of forgiveness and transformation may take many forms and occur over many years. It is usually not linear but circular in nature as we visit and revisit chapters of our life and find the ability to see compassion in those who participated in those passages with us.

3. **Last, we must be willing to do the work of** *reintegration.* Reintegration means that we take what we have learned from our separation and our transformation and bring these gifts back into the world we have come from in new ways. This giving of this gift will provide great healing, *especially in the lives within the circle of our family*. Although our return home may ultimately look different from what we imagine, our journey of family healing will most likely be more of an inward journey than an outward one.

In my own journey, I have come to appreciate the story and analogies of the prodigal son and its parallels to the hero's journey – how he experienced his separation, transformation and return. Being banished or lost from our home and family, squandering and then finding ourselves, and ultimately discovering a new path home are part of a process common to many cultural archetypes and religious rituals and stories.

Webster's dictionary defines *prodigal* as "to drive away or squander." The act of *squandering*, although certainly not good in its intention, can create a necessary void in our lives. When we are willing to recognize and learn from this void, it can carry with it many gifts. Should we have the fortune to recognize and reclaim what has been squandered or lost, we are given a wonderful opportunity to reshape it into the gift or *boon* that we can bring home and give back to those we love.

If we embrace our journey, and the moments of passage that at first might feel the most difficult, and *answer the call*, we become pliable and open to new roads and ways of being that allow us to better express our gifts within the world and our life.

For me, this experience came when I was faced with six months of treatment for breast cancer. What I collected along the way was a deep reflection of my own family passage, which when framed in the treatment for cancer, was transformed into a new story. For decades, I had absorbed the stresses of my family's trials into my little body the way a strong building endures an earthquake. Prior to my experience with cancer, there was little I did not emotionally ingest. I took a certain pride in my unflinching ability to soak up whatever difficulty came my way.

When confronted with the cancer diagnosis and treatment plan, however, I became acutely aware of how I, in fact, had *squandered* so many of my own gifts. I had become like a French drain — always able to take on the overflow. The gifts that I had received as a birthright had been buried so deep inside me for so long that they felt lost to me. With the diagnosis, my effort to be the suckling breast for everyone and everything around me reached its limits. I was left naked and stripped of my over-nurturing exuberance and ground down to my purest essence, barely able to care for myself, let alone all those around me. I realized that my nurturing was not nurturing at all. Facing this truth was *the separation* on my own hero's journey.

I was confronted with the truth that if we are to transform our strained family relationships, we must remove ourselves from the unhealthy pattern with which we have related to one another. We must, in fact, surrender to all three necessary phases of the hero's passage: separation, transformation, and reintegration.

For me, the suckling breast had become diseased both literally and symbolically. I had lived for years in a constant state of giving with no refueling mechanism in place. As a result, my body had reached its own "peak oil" crisis, and it was time for a new energy model — one that was sustainable and supported my whole being in mind, body, and spirit. My understanding of this part of myself that I gained from undergoing the treatment for cancer was the transformation on my journey, and by gaining this understanding I was able to begin to build a new model of relating to those I loved.

This new model of course would allow me to return home to my family in a new way. But what would this look like? The new paradigm looks different for each of us; the father who awaits our return may take many forms. But it was my own ability to make peace in my heart with the people I was born to that vibrated true of a family healed.

Shamanic Initiations

For all of the talk among spiritual experts that a traumatic passage through depression, addiction, loss, or illness is not necessary to find a return to your lost self, these experiences are often vital to our humility and willingness to answer the call. These experiences, once they are recognized for what they are, become the portals to our journey of self-discovery. In many native cultures, such an experience is referred to as a *shamanic initiation* — a rite of passage that, although not planned, provides as powerful a rite as its ritualized counterpart. It is because they are not planned that shamanic initiations are both powerful and interesting. It is as if the universe finds us unable to learn the lessons we are meant to learn on our own, so we are instead instilled with an experience from the outside to provide us with the growth we need.

Many of us can identify with the prodigal son's story, following a desire to leave the life in which we were raised to seek out a reality that more closely aligns with our authenticity. We may even have been fortunate enough to find a moment of real awakening and a return to ourselves on this journey. Ironically, however, it is once reunited with our true essence that we are often met with an unrelenting desire to return home. Suddenly we realize that our authenticity includes the family we grew up in. They were not just a reflection of our false life - they were part of who we really were all along. Yet it is this return home that is often the most difficult as we revisit relationships with family members who are far away, emotionally unavailable or even no longer with us. As we contemplate the challenges of such a return, we may want to consider the following:

What we leave on the table with our family relationships may well prove to be some of the most powerful and spiritually healing material available to us during our earthly journey - our grist for the soul mill. As with the prodigal son, the role our family has played in our life is an important one and what our family brings out in us offers us great opportunities for further personal growth. They are at the heart of our learning, essential to the 'soulular' transformations that we came here to embody. As we trace and even rebuild these connections, we may come to see and appreciate these individuals as members of our own spiritual Olympic team on our journey here on Earth.

Unfortunately, not all family members may be interested in (or capable) of joining us on this trip home. The first time around within the family may have been enough for them; they may choose to continue on their path with new people, leaving the relationships and experiences of the past behind them. They may even find new people who serve as buffers between them and their old family, as an insurance policy against recreating these relationships. We need to respect that our own family members are on their own journeys, and *their* journeys may be in the transformative stages, not yet ready to return to us, as we might wish they would.

As with any emotional work, we cannot coerce others to meet us where we now stand. We can, however, create a standing invitation in our own hearts. We can extend to our family members an acceptance and forgiveness that honors the place where they are on their own journeys. It is not always for us to understand or interpret the events of another person's life and how those events may unfold and serve him or her.

By practicing this "honoring," we can learn a new way of love and compassion for those who may never have understood us and may even have hurt us. It is the love and compassion that we have so often sought desperately for ourselves in our own interactions with them. We cannot coax them home; we can only offer the gift of our acceptance and love.

By recognizing and understanding the *faulty code* that may have been handed down to us and our children, we can change what our

61

family has believed, even for centuries, to be true and embrace a new and more healthy understanding of what it means to be a "family."

Through this process of reawakening not only our true self, but the often lost stories of our past, we find that when we answer the call, our life may shift from that moment on. We may receive a new understanding of why God dropped us into this unique group of people and discover the amazing gifts that can be realized by openly and honestly revisiting the stories of our own family.

Removing Ourselves from the Tree

The privilege of a lifetime is being who you are.
  - Joseph Campbell, *Reflections on the Art of Living*

Campbell's model taught me that if we are to be the architects of our own lives, we must be willing to *hear* and *answer the call* on our own journey. The call may come to us in many ways. But primarily, it comes to us in the form of discomfort. It lets us know that something is not right; our interactions with our family of origin, especially into adulthood, serve as moments to hear the call that beckons us.

Traditional family therapy defines removing ourselves emotionally and physically from our family as "emotional cut-off" — and for many family members it is often the only safe and viable option. When maintaining our existing role in the family dynamic no longer serves any useful or healthy process, emotional cut-off, as negative as it may sound, can be a great time of growth and self-discovery — gifting us with new ways of seeing ourselves, our lives, and enabling us to choose new life partners, friends, and even extended family members. We can create new patterns that offer healthier possibilities for our human relationships.

About six years into my own marriage, it became evident to me that the strain I was experiencing in trying constantly to integrate the culture of my family of origin with the new family Rich and I had created in California was fraying my nerves. We were just barely able to care for our three small children, maintain our house and our growing business. I came to realize that whenever there was an interaction between my California family and my relatives, there was a tension in my mind between who I was with Rich and my kids and who I was with my family of origin.

Years later, I was able to find some space by limiting my contact with my family of origin for a period of time. As I kept the interactions at a minimum, I got more and more comfortable with the person I was becoming and began to get to know myself, my husband, and my kids in new ways.

Emotional cut-off offers us a chance to regroup and reclaim the self that was lost under the false self we created during our childhood years. It creates a void that presents us with new opportunity for questioning, exploring, and healing the ills of the past.

We can only imagine what the prodigal son's life would have looked like had he never left home. Imagine for a moment that he depleted his entire family fortune; his squandering could have become an endless activity. Who would he have become? Who would his family have been? How would his father have been able to embrace him had the son not had the opportunity to find his own way and experience the world through his own set of eyes?

In many other cultures, leaving home and going out on our own is done at the age of thirteen. In such cultures and where adolescents have a healthy experience of this, a true passage can be realized. In situations where this is not the case, adolescence may be played out in later life (in some cases much later life), at a time when it feels awkward and uncomfortable. But know that the journey away from home and removing ourselves from the family tree may be a natural and necessary step in our self-discovery and in our ability to bring back to our family the ultimate gift of our truest self.

A Love of Fear and Fear of Love

> *We sometimes live as if only survival were real, as if our only resources were reptilian. That is where war, retaliation, and aggression can take the reins. As humans we are inherently loving, but fear can prevent that love from arising.*
>
> *- David Richo, Five Things We Cannot Change*

Love is the natural state of the human condition. This concept has been all but lost in our culture as we have been trained and programmed by nearly everything around us to believe otherwise. The understanding of this truth and our willingness to embrace it are critical instruments in our ability to change the emotional direction of our lives.

The "fight-or-flight response" was first described in 1915 by the American psychologist Walter Cannon as a way to define how animals respond under stress. Since then, the model has been used widely by our medical establishment as a measurement for how the human body functions under extreme and often prolonged stress and how such stress can affect such functions as heart health and blood pressure. The "fight-or-flight response" has become the way that most of us now live.

Many of us, from the moment we wake up, are submerged in a world of fear and hence stress. A typical day for many of us might include the following:

We wake in the morning and go online to check our bank account, only to find out money was moved into the wrong account. We then spend an hour on the phone waiting for and receiving assistance to fix the problem. Later, we learn that, despite our efforts to set ourselves up for the best plan, our cellular bill went over by 200 minutes and we will be charged an additional .45 a minute; another hour on the phone. There are three separate afterschool activities the kids need to be driven to, so we forgo our hopeful plan for a family dinner at home and spend three hours battling the local traffic. All of these events take place in the gaps between living our regular life, going to work, and taking care of our bodies.

By 7:00 in the evening, we fall onto the couch and turn on the TV news. We hear how much more unstable the world has become since the day before, as the network tries to keep us plugged in while they meet advertising revenue targets. By 9:00 p.m., we are exhausted, irritated with our kids, but too anxious to get any good sleep. Lucky to undress and brush our teeth, we throw ourselves down for our restless sleep and then wake to get up and do it all again.

I used to tell Rich when our kids were little that I would lie in bed in the morning for a few extra moments to just avoiding getting on "the ride." I knew the minute I put my clothes on and entered the hallway, the adrenaline would begin, along with the day. It would not stop until I was back under the covers later that night.

This is not a condition the human body was meant to endure on a daily basis. Yet we have all become comfortable with this way of life — a whole new sense of normal.

Knowing this, is there any reason to spend any energy revisiting the relationships of our family of origin? Our parents did their damage; why should we invite them back into our lives during this most crazy time just to have them remind us we are "not doing it right?" This would certainly not provide any ointment for the wound.

But the truth is we cannot heal any of these ills in our lives until we start to listen to the messages of our body. Our body speaks the truth. It carries in it all the stories of trauma, neglect, hurt, and difficulty that we have endured. With our over-individualized sense of self, we have, on top of all this, burdened ourselves with the impossible task of "getting over it and moving on" and dish out to ourselves heavy, heavy doses of guilt and self-criticism when we are unable to do so.

As David Berceli points out in his book, *the Revolutionary Trauma Release Process*, we are all living organisms on this planet. Yet as human beings we have found a way to falsely exempt ourselves from this equation. We have become deeply confused as a species about our connection to the natural world and are almost overwhelmed with our sense of spiritual awareness — we don't know quite what to do with it. Of all the species on the planet, we are the only one who has become a predator onto ourselves. We have seen in the past century more deaths within our species at our own hands — a self-inflicted trauma that we keep perpetuating again and again — than any other time in history.

When we face a typical stressful day, the fight-or-flight chemicals in our bodies kick in at higher and higher rates. We are "charged" with these chemicals without a way to release them. Typically, we return to our home after a long, stressful day with the intention to relax. Instead, many of us find openings in which to gradually release these overcharged chemicals and emotions, tragically, onto the people we love. We walk around with an unconscious rationalization that this is somehow appropriate, that this is the environment where we are meant to relax, and we find no issue with snapping at our spouse or children for not doing what they are supposed to be doing on the *team family*.

How distant the family model has become from its romanticized image. We get married and have children with the best intentions. We hope for a nest of love, and we create instead many times a den of pain. How can we relinquish our tendency to relate from a place of fear and once again safely connect in a loving way with the people we share our life and home with? How can we rebuild the bridge and make our home the true haven it was meant to be — providing a real feeling of peace, nurturing, and safety from the stresses of the outside world?

Much of this, I believe, lies in rethinking our way of interacting with our family members and taking a close and honest look at how we treat each other. For many of us, if we were to look honestly at our home lives, we would realize that we often treat our coworkers, bartenders, college buddies, dental hygienists, and auto mechanics better than we treat our family members. We say "Please" and "Thank you" more to strangers and people on the outer circles of our life than we do to our own siblings, parents, and children.

As we decrease the number of waking moments in our lives we spend engaged in fear, we increase the amount of time spent in a state of love. A move back into this place requires from us two things:

First, we must be willing to wake with the sun each day and fall into bed each night acknowledging to ourselves that "love is the natural state of the human condition."

Second, we must be willing to commit to the journey of finding a way back to this state.

This is not a small task. As we interact on many levels with many people throughout our day, we need to become aware of how we treat people — both inside and outside our home. With a little effort, we can see that making small changes in how we treat people can have a huge effect. A simple "Please" or "Thank you" or even mustering up a smile when we might not otherwise do so can change the mood of our entire day.

Many of the teachings of Christianity are centered on the art of interacting from a place of love, empathy, and compassion. The practice of such a way of life, however, requires us to relinquish something that has for many people become a dear, dear friend: *fear*. Fear and the aggressiveness and protectionism it carries as its constant companions are for many of us the primary modes of functioning in our daily lives.

During one of the 2008 presidential debates, then-Senator Barack Obama referred to John McCain's approach to removing many government programs like using a hammer instead of a scalpel.

The fear in our toolbox is like the hammer used in this analogy. And although you might not consider yourself a "fearful" person, consider the approach you take when protecting yourself. We often pride ourselves on our ability to "stick up for ourselves" in conflict. When we feel threatened, we believe we have a right to respond in an equally aggressive or threatening way. *Not* sticking up for ourselves can not only be *frightening*, but it may not even make sense within the context of the world in which we live. What we need to rebuild our family and other relationships is not a hammer *or* a scalpel, but a paintbrush, a pen, a warm blanket, and possibly a good pot to make soup in.

If you are like many people, fear has served you well for many years. It has protected you through difficult times and through many perceived threats. The truth is, that as Franklin D. Roosevelt said, we truly do have nothing to fear but fear itself.

We can fear the natural disasters of the world, but is there any value in keeping ourselves jacked up about it? If we live on the fault line in California or the hurricane path in New Orleans, does it help us in anyway to remain in a heightened state of anxiety as we go through our day and complete our other earthly tasks?

By keeping our protective layer and continuing to interact in a state of heightened alert, we perpetuate a world in which there is still something we *perceive* as warranting both fear and its aggressive response. We become like little people in the bumper cars at the fair, each of us bumping and bouncing off one another, with a mini-traumatic jolt amping us up for the next collision. With our protective bumpers, our human interactions have become more like "collisions" than exchanges. Whether we are getting gas or buying a coffee or checking out of the market with our groceries, we tend to look upon these interactions as almost two dimensional, with the person we are interacting with is serving a function for us, not unlike our computers, dishwashers, cars, and telephones. We have reduced the very people God has put in our path throughout the day to objects.

Understanding the role our love of fear and fear of love play in the potential to rebuild our families is fundamental. If we start with the outer circle, the one that is the least "charged" with energy, we can use this realm to experiment with a new way of looking at our lives. Gradually, we can work our way inward, to the other circles.

Family and Post-Traumatic Stress "Mind" Fields

What we must come to realize is that we are living in an organism that will continually repeat some form of the trauma until it can successfully release the residual energy and restore itself to a healthy and calm state. The urge to repeat the trauma through re-enactment is so severe and compulsive because the drive to complete this discharge of excess energy is so vital for the body's healthy functioning. It must restore itself to its healthiest possible state to assure the survival of our species.
  - David Berceli, *The Revolutionary Trauma Release Process*

As Americans, we live in one of the most diverse countries in the world. More than any other country on the planet, the United States offers people a place to come where they can become someone their previous country or culture would not allow them to be. For many foreigners, coming to the United States is like having the chance to build the house of bricks, and the wolf at the door — an oppressive government or inopportune economy — is left behind and burned in the caldron of the past and replaced with the hope of a new life and family culture.

For many, the first new generation is like the genealogical honeymoon. From oppressed lands and lives, immigrants enter the United States to create the existence they have always dreamed of. They raise their children with a new freedom not previously available to them. Most first-generation families do not take these gifts lightly.

As with all great change, however, something is lost, and for many immigrant families that loss often involves the fabric of extended family. Leaving relatives in other countries can include lost generations of aunts, uncles, cousins, and grandparents — a change in the dynamic that forever resets the family and its history and often leaves a splintered new picture — a "fractal" or smaller split-off version of what the family once was.

Both my husband and my college roommate are first-generation Americans — my husband has one and my college roommate has two parents who came here from another country. My own father's family came to the states when my father was a teenager

70

from Canada. Not all that different a culture, but the family splintering was as powerful nonetheless.

How do families deal with such splintering? How does a daughter or son process the guilt of leaving behind the parents who raised him or her? How does someone let the memory of a faraway grandparent or aunt or uncle live on — however painful or unhealthy the life left behind may have been?

Often this splintering is incorporated and absorbed into the new family by sustaining the "spirit" of these lost family members in their new family relationships. *This unconscious embodiment of honoring lost family members often helps relieve the guilt of leaving them behind.* And through this embodiment, the new family is "haunted" with the ways of the old family, even though they may be thousands and thousands of miles away.

The human psyche often has a hard time completely cutting the umbilical chord from the family of origin or culture of the past; often it must instead find ways to integrate these old family ways into its new family life. This occurs despite the fact that for many, the dysfunction of the old family played a major role in why they fled to begin with.

As a result of this, many first- and second-generation Americans experience what I call the family *posttraumatic stress "mind" field.* As the stress from these separations begin to take shape, we may recognize traumatic experiences we have been through in our childhood but sense that they have little to do with us or even our parents. Yet the interactions and expressions of just such feelings can be intense and cause us great pain later in life as we continue to feel them but have little information or understanding of there origins.

The sixth of eight kids in a half-Irish and half-Iranian family, my husband has three older brothers. When I have spent time with two or more of them together over the years, I have often felt that the energy field around them could be felt blocks away. I have witnessed interactions where Rich and his brothers have triggered in each other many behaviors, feelings and memories of the past, often unknowingly and even unconsciously. With one of his brothers, these interactions have been at times sprinkled with moments where the two of them have inadvertently stepped on one another's hearts as a result of these emotional time travels. Like the bull in the china shop, there are often too many breakable objects that have been left exposed from the years of being raised in such a highly competitive

71

environment that some of these exchanges have turned less than peaceful.

These moments have been particularly heart wrenching for me, as I have seen the magic that can flow between them when they are allowed to be their carefree and truest selves. But when they accidentally slip into wounded territory, the *mind fields* can be big and explosive, and have even at times warranted a complete time-out from one another — often for extended periods of time.

When our interactions with family members cause us to operate from a heightened sense of alert, it becomes obvious that we have not had a chance to properly *release the trauma of the past*. In some large families, where there have been great stresses and hardships, it can even become hard to remember the roots of these feelings and the experiences that initially triggered them. But if they are not given the space to heal, they will forever be reopened in the presence of those who subconsciously serve as reminders to us of these moments.

The explosiveness of the post-traumatic stress mind field is one of the loudest calls we can receive to address these deep wounds. We must not only treat them with a separation from those who keep reopening them, but also allow them the proper dressing and sunlight to let them finally heal. When they do heal, we may one day return to the original places where they were inflicted, and only scars will be found on our skin. Through a grown-up compassion and love and a deep understanding and realization that we were not the only one who sustained such injuries, we can introduce a healing to our family that can be felt for generations to come.

Certainly the prodigal son could not have returned to his father's house had he not completed the full cycle of separation and transformation. He could return home only under the circumstances that he did.

For many of us, even this may be a fantasy never fulfilled. We must befriend our wounds and understand what reopens them. We must remember that when a grown sibling or a parent is able to reduce us to a state of panic or deep pain, they are not the villain but simply the messenger, reminding us of how deeply we were hurt and how alive these wounds still are. They are inviting us to return to our second circle and reacquaint ourselves with the shadows that live there and the peace we need to make with them.

The Nature of Nonreconciliation

As long as you are in a state of vulnerability, you must not attempt to perform miracles.

- A Course in Miracles

Nonreconciliation is a way that people relate to one another after years of reinforced behavior when forgiveness feels too threatening even to entertain. Nonreconciled relationships are very sophisticated and involve a high amount of *other* blame; each person finds ways to credit the other person with their own sense of discomfort and unhappiness.

These patterns develop early in relationships, usually under the first stressful episode that the relationship undergoes, but they can be refined into an entire way of relating. In a therapy session in my early twenties, the therapist told me that one of the biggest reasons that people stay married to each other is to have someone to blame for life's disappointments.

Shame and blame, the fabric that often holds families together, creates a large and powerful energy field that any member will have a difficult time releasing themselves from. Such a culture can take over the entire identity of the family and parents may use the shame and blame techniques to shield themselves from any ownership of their less than successful efforts at raising a family, or the stresses they have endured from feeling inadequate in providing their children the love and emotional acceptance they crave.

In the story of the return of the prodigal son, there are two important components to the reconciliation: humility *and* forgiveness. Without either one of these two ingredients, reconciliation is not possible. In the story, the father shows us an almost celebratory display of forgiveness in response to his son's abundant humility and ability to return to both his true self *and* his family.

There are many variations on this story that would not have culminated in the celebratory reconciliation. If the son had not found his bottom, or not returned home, or if the father had instead sent him away or made him beg for reentry into the family — any of these variations would have kept the family in a deadlock of nonreconciliation for generations to come.

In most families, there are many moments of reconciliation that go unrealized. We are often so busy keeping score, punishing, competing, and protecting ourselves that the tiny seeds that could blossom into true moments of forgiveness and awakening are left as silenced voices, unheard in the loud and clamoring noise of self-protection.

We cannot control others' choice to forgive. But we can recognize them when they occur, and be willing and eager to participate in them. These moments may not present themselves as revelations of self but as small but humble admissions. The important thing is that we are prepared for them. If, for instance, we are holding a longstanding resentment toward someone in our family and he or she shares a humble moment and asks our forgiveness for something recent or years past, our immediate response may be to *use* this moment of weakness to leverage our own power and strengthen our position of defensiveness with them. When we have not prepared for such moments, we will be unable to forgive when they are given to us. If we have not made peace with ourselves and become truly grounded in our heart and truer self, the acceptance of this act of humility will be virtually impossible.

This is a pattern I have seen again and again in families. Someone begins to shift from a hardened position on an issue (or even about themselves) and will begin to reach out. The receiving family member may often not only not be prepared for this change of heart but rebuff it as insincere or even threatening. "We must be strong and tough in our family" is the thought. Why should we change our culture? Why should we soften when all of our family's strength has been built on challenging each other and demanding so much from one another?

An Exercise in Preparing for Forgiveness

One way to move away from a family culture of nonreconciliation is to prepare ourselves for just such an event. This can be done by first taking a emotional inventory of our relationships with each of our family members and how we feel toward them, and begin to look at ways we can find forgiveness with them within our own hearts. This step is essential if we are to change anything in our relationship with them.

One way you can do this by writing down the family member's name on a piece of paper or the back of a business card. Do this in a quiet space, with at least five or ten minute of time, and see what comes up. You can imagine that you need to place a phone call to them, or that you need to drive or fly to their house and show up unannounced at their front door. What are the feelings that this moment brings up for you? How do you imagine yourself feeling when you must speak to them or show up at their house unannounced? As unnatural as this may at first seem, this is the first seed of reconciliation. You have now invoked an intention of forgiveness and are inviting this person to be part of your life in a new way. You need to think about them many times throughout the day, and when you do, you can begin to try the simple exercise of remembering that there is a very good chance that they are living with a very similar sense of the fear and angst that plagues your side of the relationship.

You may want to take this small card or piece of paper and keep it in your wallet. As you go throughout your day and find yourself in a particularly peaceful or joyous moment, bring the card out and speak the person's name. As you start to bring her or him into your consciousness when you are in a positive and compassionate place, your sense of resentment may begin to fade.

As you will see through more specific exercises in chapter 6, the processes of forgiveness, finding humility, and ultimately reconciliation begins with you. Your work and your gift to your family may not involve picking up the phone or sending a note; the work may need to take place inside your own heart. If you can find ways to incorporate a physical symbol of the person you are working with into your life and find moments throughout your day to honor her, a movement of forgiveness may eventually come over your relationship, like melting ice in spring.

This cannot happen without conscious thought and attention, but it will shift with some time and true intention. We oftentimes will try to force changes in these relationships before we are ready, throwing ourselves into the relationship, trying to fix it through a physical drive, a sense of guilt or obligation, rather than from the compass of our own heart.

4. Healing and Forgiveness

If we practice an eye for an eye and a tooth for a tooth, soon the whole world will be blind and toothless.

- Mahatma Gandhi

Behind a thin veil of all anger and resentment lies forgiveness. People whom you have met may share stories of how they were suddenly overcome with a deep sense of peace in their lives. The most important component to this sense of peace, I can promise you, was most likely forgiveness. *Forgiveness* —the word itself contains the word *give*. We cannot love another human being or even ourselves fully without practicing forgiveness on a regular basis.

Although the translation of the Greek word *sin* that is used often in our culture and throughout the Bible involves wrongdoing, some scholars have opted for the more literal translation of it as simply "missing the mark." This is a subtle difference, but an important one, because if we are to think of sin in this way, it implies a vacuum rather than the presence of something specifically not good. The absence of or "missing the mark" implies instead that we have drifted or deviated from our true essence, the essence of love. When we act *not* out of love, but from any other place or motivation, we are acting out of sin. When we lose our place in the core of our soul, the place from which God endowed us with the ability to understand how connected we all really are, we lose our connectedness not just to one another but to ourselves. When we stay connected with and function only from our hearts, sin becomes virtually impossible. It is very difficult to perform any of the "though shall not" acts from the commandments when we have both our own and another person's best intentions at heart.

For these reasons, we reframe forgiveness as the place we must return to when we want to let go of our bitterness and anger toward others. The reason I say at the opening of the chapter that forgiveness lies hidden behind only a *thin* veil is that when we return to ourselves and to our hearts, we return to what is real, and all else falls away. When we accept that *all sin* is committed from a place of *separation from the heart* and rejoin with our own heart, we take an important step toward forgiveness for both ourselves and the other souls we interact with.

Why Forgiveness Is So Confusing

Made direct amends to such people wherever possible, except when to do so would injure them or others.

Step 9 – Alcoholics Anonymous, *The Big Book*

There are many fallacies and misconceptions about forgiveness, how available it is to us, and what it requires us to do. As a result, many of us abandon efforts or intentions of forgiveness for fear of being wounded again.

As we delicately thread the needle of forgiveness, it will require from us that we look at ourselves and others in a pure and innocent light, abandoning many of our old ways of thinking. Forgiveness for many is a scary thing; it can conjure up images of falling, letting go, and even careening of control. Sometimes our sense of anger and bitterness toward others gives us a false sense of safety —if we remain angry at them, we build a protective cocoon inside which we remain untouched by any further hurt.

One aspect of remaining in a state of nonforgiveness that we often overlook is the toll it takes on our own spirit. The psychological and emotional effort required to maintain feelings of anger toward another human being is not a passive act. It requires us to wake each day and reinvoke these feelings, and keep them upheld and maintained. We then release specific stress-induced chemicals into our body during our brain's vigil to perpetuate this state of aggression.

So how, then, do we reconcile our own need for safety and protection with our desire to forgive and move our own spirit and body back into a state of peace? It is this question that leaves so many of us confused about forgiveness and often abandoning our efforts toward it altogether.

Forgiveness for Breakfast, Lunch, and Dinner

Without anxiety the mind is wholly kind, and because it extends beneficence it is beneficent. Safety is the complete relinquishment of attack.

A Course in Miracles

An important step we can take in our efforts toward forgiveness of another person is to imagine for a moment a relationship with him or her that is bathed in safety. We have to look hard at what this means. It may, in fact, mean we do not have any physical contact with the person. It may mean we do not speak to him, but in our hearts, we make a new safe space for him. In this step, we open a new place for him in our life that is not threatening to us, and we can begin to look at the person with a new set of eyes and a more loving heart.

Once we have begun to feel what it would be like to have this person in our hearts in a nonthreatening way, we can start to look at the interaction we have had with him and where he might have felt threatened or wounded. As you begin to revisit certain events in your life, particularly traumatic unresolved family conflicts, you may find new ways to look at these events if you are willing to move the person or persons involved in these conflicts into a safe and nonthreatening place in your heart. You may need also to give yourself license to not interact with this person while you pass through this change of heart.

As you go through your day, allow yourself to revisit the person in your mind and heart, and when he comes up, imagine him as a small child. Then imagine that the same wounding experiences that have left you protective and unable to access your own love and true essence have also affected them. Imagine how they might be different in their character and core and how their protective and defensive mechanisms may have played a different role in how they, too, had to process and absorb these experiences.

Separating yourself from this family member can be an important part of the process of creating a more healthy sense of differentiation, of realizing that you are separate persons, and each of you has had to process and absorb painful and often traumatic events of the faulty code that was handed down.

Whether this person is a sibling, parent, or child, it is likely that you are both dealing with similar energy and past events, but you are simply processing it through a different lens. But by beginning to understand that you are *both* victims of the same falsehoods, you can start the process of forgiveness by seeing the person through more empathetic eyes.

Forgiveness and Grace

Healing is of God in the end.
A Course in Miracles

When we begin the shift to a more compassionate, empathetic, and loving view of a family member, we often reach an impasse or place where we get stuck. Some of the confrontations or events we have shared may be so painful that our bodies have not fully processed them, or they remain lodged in a part of our brain or psyche where we do not yet have full access to them.

At this point, we must recognize an important component to forgiveness: grace. Grace may conjure up many things for us, but I refer to *grace* here as an awakening, a new perspective or shift in our mind and heart that is *not directly under our control.* For people who have suffered severe family trauma, this can be one of the most difficult concepts to grasp.

Grace is particularly important in families who have experienced pain and trauma because the recognition and acceptance of grace is also the recognition of forces outside of ourselves working in a positive way. Each time an act of grace is acknowledged, we begin to rebuild our lost sense of trust in the world, our family, and ourselves.

The more you begin to acknowledge and become sensitive to acts of grace in your presence, the more such acts will be revealed to you. The more they are shown to you, the faster and more effortless the work around forgiveness will become.

Becoming an Ambassador of Love

And there are those who have little and give it all.
- Kahlil Gibran, The Prophet

No relationship can be healed while we remain in a place where we are in need of something from it. The only true way to begin healing in any relationship, including those with members of our family, is by making our every action about giving. Once we succumb to our desire to make the reconciliation focused on what we *need* — what we perceive we are not getting from someone else — we are disconnected from the healing energy and lost from the new path of reconciliation we have so bravely put ourselves on.

Beyond the fact that giving is a key ingredient in healing, there is a hidden gift in the family reconciliation process as it relates to giving. Kahlil Gibran, in his words on giving, recognizes that those who have little give it all. It is the *little* that needs to be given in order that it may grow and be shared.

When our journey to reunite ourselves with our true essence takes us to a place where we can rediscover ourselves, we may be met with resistance from our family. However, when we are able to *give* from this new place, the essence of who we are will be harder to resist. Equally, the more we give from this part of ourselves, the stronger it becomes, and the more grounded and centered we become in our inner circle. This is why it is so important to think of all your interactions and acts of healing with family members *only* as acts of giving.

As you may have begun to experience, *giving* is the true healing energy, and there is nothing you need in return other than the realization that you already have everything you need. The more you share this realization with those you love, the more you increase the possibility of them finding their way home as well.

The Priest, the Nurse, and the Prodigal Father

Being deeply loved by someone gives you strength, while loving someone deeply gives you courage.

- Lao Tzu

One of the aspects of my experience with chemotherapy that struck me was how much patience and giving is involved in the treatment of cancer. While patients sit passively in large chairs receiving drips of chemotherapy, nurses attend and respond diligently to the most subtle changes or circumstances.

When taking a type of chemo called Taxol that is so toxic it is capable of triggering an extreme allergic reaction, I was required to take in intravenous dose of steroids and Benadryl prior to receiving it. The combination of these drugs would put me in a very sleepy state. After a couple hours of being in the chair, I began to drift off into a light sleep, only to be gently awakened by a nurse who sensed from the color of my cheeks that I "didn't look right." She immediately took me off of the chemo drip and administered a second dose of the steroids and Benadryl, suspecting I was having an allergic reaction to the Taxol.

What impressed me about this interaction was the diligence, care, and sensitivity of the nurse who was watching over me. I think of these nurses often and am always inspired by their gentle nature and their entire days spent simply giving. They watch each person in the chemo ward closely for any signs that he or she may need something, be it a simple thing like an extra pillow or a cup of tea. They move from one chair to the next, checking on their patients like a mother hen checks on and counts her chicks. The role of the nurse is a completely selfless role; they are administering, in addition to the chemotherapy, love.

I believe that real healing in the body occurs more quickly and more fully in the presence of love, and my time on the chemo ward is a testament to this. There was never a day that I did not leave the floor feeling completely inspired and moved by the stories I would hear from other patients or by the sensitive and compassionate acts of the oncology staff.

The level of grace that went on in that small room never ceased to amaze me. Each of us hooked up to a small bag of poison for hours at a time while we were gently and lovingly attended to by the nurses. While there were a few brief moments of complaining and rebellion, the general mood of the environment was that of respect — respect for the disease, for the treatment, for the staff there all day so patiently assisting in the process, and a respect for one another.

My husband attended every session with me and was equally although differently affected by these teachings; he too got to experience the awe of watching people who were slow-dancing with the other side maintain a level of integrity and grace that was almost unimaginable. But for both of us, the trips to the chemo ward were like regularly scheduled lessons in respect and love. Simple ways of interacting once taken for granted were re-experienced in a new light. Conversations around family and children and our life stories were shared and received with new colors and levels of interest.

The entire process taught me that healing of any kind requires two elements: unyielding patience and love. There is no guarantee that by administering these two elements that healing will come, but without them, we set up a situation where we make them unlikely.

Some time after completing my treatment, I began attending classes at my local church for RCIA — the Rite of Christian Initiation of Adults. RCIA classes provide adult education to those who are considering joining the Catholic Church. I would spend more than a year in these classes preparing for baptism and communion in the Catholic Church.

The specific combination of these two experiences – the cancer treatment and my participation in RCIA - provided me with an interesting set of rituals and new ways of being. I learned a new way to see and treat people, different from any way I had experienced human interactions before.

As I simultaneously continued my recovery from the chemo and the radiation and began my classes at the church, I believed God had created for me an educational plan that I could not have created for myself. I felt like I'd been shot out of a cannon and was eager and excited to have a place in the world to share my new discoveries and continue to learn and grow.

What the nurses from the chemo ward and the priest teaching my RCIA class had in common was their unyielding and patient commitment to love. Each of them understood that to assist people in their journeys of healing required their remaining steadfast to the ideals of patience and love. Anyone who has been called to the journey of healing needs a support network of at least one other human being who keeps them grounded in the truth that *no healing is possible in the absence of love*. The priest knew this. The oncology nurses knew this. And the prodigal father knew this.

When we can bear witness to another soul's journey of being lost, being found, and coming home, we validate this process in a way that makes it solid. We cannot rush or force an awakening. We can only sit in quiet patience for their return home, just as the father did for his prodigal son.

We must always remember that when we light a candle for the return to love and to harmonious relations of those we love, we are the nurse, we are the priest, and we are the father, preparing a place that will be met with great joy and celebration.

5. Coming Home

Your daily life is your temple and your religion.
                                    - Kahlil Gibran, *The Prophet*

Reclaiming your family will require time and nurturing. It also requires a series of steps to shed what is not working (and is not based in love) and to institute new habits that will take your family to a new place.

But more important, if you are able to see yourself not only as a grownup, free of the role of child in your own family, but also as a parent and a teacher, the generation you are now raising will receive many of the gifts of your conscious and courageous journey. You will experience the challenging but joyful role of the *grown-up you* raising your own family.

Rich and I have learned many lessons over the years through our own attempts to tame the great beast of the runaway family. Neither of us had what we would have considered our ideal model from which we could directly learn how to create our own family structure one day. Much of what we have learned has been through our own trial and error. Each of us continues to struggle with our own passage from adolescence to adulthood while our own children continue to grow. Instinctually and through our daily actions, each of us knows that we can never really let up on either effort. Our passion to raise our children with the utmost sense of integrity, balance, and self-appreciation has kept us motivated and inspired.

We are always trying to find new ways to push back against our culture's growing tide of fragmented activities and stimulation and carve out small places in our lives and days to be together.

Setting Our Parents Free to Heal

Begin to configure other people as fellow pilgrims, not as shrines meant to give you comfort or answers.

- David Richo, *Five Things We Cannot Change*

As summarized in Judith Wallerstein's epic work, *The Unexpected Legacy of Divorce,* children of divorce for the most part get through their childhoods intact. Like a cancer patient who puts on her coat of bravery to undergo chemotherapy, we put aside the ill effects and post-traumatic moments for a safer, quieter time when the horrors can surface (sometimes only subconsciously) into our reality. Adult children of divorce usually see the emotional wounds of their parents' divorce only later, when they begin the creation of their own families.

The legacy that is left from many years of avoiding conflict or commitment that many children of divorce are left with can feel like trying to see in the dark on a very foggy night with dim headlights. We strain to see what ills inflict us that are not even our own.

But if we look deep enough, we can claim these free-floating emotional radicals as our own and then release them. We can do this by meditating deeply on all the thoughts our subconscious is holding around our parents, who they are, and what they have endured. We most likely know more about our parents than we think we know or that we acknowledge to ourselves. The secret here, however, is to release them from the role of "parent" in our mind's eye and look at them as people —God's children, like ourselves. This shift in how we see our parents can lead us to a better understanding of both our families and the histories they have endured.

Once we can see our parents clearly, as fellow souls on the planet, we can look at them deeply, with a sense of empathy, and imagine who they are, all they have been through, and the pressures they have endured on their journeys. If all else fails, you can meditate on this as their gift to you. Whatever false sense of power we have developed by believing that we completely control our own destiny, the fact cannot be denied that we cannot birth ourselves onto the planet. Only God and our parents had a hand in this event, and whatever ills our parents have delivered onto us, this simple fact cannot be denied.

A Meditation Exercise

Begin the meditation simply and let the idea wash over you that they, too, started out with faulty code. They were given the role of parent or husband or wife without proper training or maturity. Think of all of the images that this conjures up. The more time you spend viewing your parent or parents in this light, the more you open yourself up to becoming their savior, should *they* ever find *their* lost selves and need a path home.

Now that you are grown, you are free to release them from the role of parent. You are free to wait patiently with an extended invitation, always ready to celebrate their journey home, should they find the courage and freedom to go there.

Grafting the Apple Tree

Love recognizes no barriers. It jumps hurdles, leaps fences, penetrates walls to arrive at its destination full of hope.

- Maya Angelou

Wikipedia defines the act of *grafting* as a method of asexual plant propagation used in agriculture and horticulture in which the tissues of one plant are encouraged to fuse with those of another.

I first learned of apple tree grafting after moving to Sonoma, while I was having breakfast at an outdoor patio at a local restaurant. Next to me, I saw an apple tree that had just been planted. On each branch was a separate identifying tag specifying the type of apples grown on the tree. One tag on one branch said Golden Delicious, the other Red Delicious. How confusing this was —had someone at the plant store mad a mistake and put too many tags on the tree?

Some weeks later, we were visiting friends in a neighboring town, and I noticed a tree with tags like this in their back yard. I asked them about it; they explained to me the process of grafting — how you take a branch from one apple tree and attach it to another tree where it would grow and prosper and produce fruit completely different from the mother tree on which it grew.

Apple tree grafting became to me a symbol of how new families are often built; the idea that this was possible gave me great hope in our ability to form new families from such disparate and culturally different groups of people. I am still fascinated by my husband's cultural blending and how his mother so gracefully took on the task of learning to prepare traditional Persian dishes, despite her own upbringing as the first generation of Irish immigrants raised in Yonkers. Rich still has fond memories of the dishes his mother would create and the smells and aromas from these dishes that would have been otherwise unknown to him had his mother not taken the time to graft this extension of her husband's food history and culture. Despite the other hardships that this family endured, she was able to hand down to another generation my husband's father's culture through one of the most important and practical forms available: cooking.

Even today, Rich and I will go to the East Bay and visit his favorite Persian delicatessen where he will purchase cookies that his grandmother used to bring from Iran. We purchased a wonderful Persian cookbook from which Rich has made many dishes. The act of preparing and enjoying these meals serves as an honoring of the best that both his parents gave to him — his father's unique cultural heritage and his mother's sensitivity and dedication to making sure her children had an understanding of it in their daily life through the food that they shared and enjoyed.

In our own family, we have grafted onto the apple tree the additional cultural aspect that our children are not only Irish and Persian in their heritage, but are also native Californians. Rich and I are often reminded of this when we take trips back east and are made aware through slight differences that our children are obviously from a different culture than many of our relatives.

I particularly love the metaphor of the grafted apple tree because it speaks to us about the potential to bring into the fold new aspects of our family, new ways and varieties of living that we can incorporate into our own families. Sometimes it is that new type of apple that can be the changing force on the tree, forever altering our family and who it is in so many ways.

In the chapter that follows, I invite you to look at some of the ways in which you have begun to feel differently about your family and if you feel ready, explore the idea of actually reaching out to one or more family members through letter writing. Letter writing, when done from a place of love, can be a wonderful way to reconnect with loved ones, especially where physical distance has been a factor in your relationship.

6. Love Letters

You often say, "I would give, but only to the deserving."
The trees in your orchard say not so, nor the flocks in your pasture.
They give that they may live, for to withhold is to perish.

　　　　　　　　　　　　　- Kahlil Gibran, *The Prophet*

What I have always loved about Princess Diana was her passion for letter and note writing. In interviews, she discussed how she would never let more than 48 hours go by without sending a thank you note to someone for anything. It was one of her golden rules. I found a true sense of graciousness in that gesture that I still carry with me today, although I often fall short on the follow-through.

The goal of this chapter is to offer a new way of sharing yourself with those closest to you and applying the five circles theory to your relationships with family members. Viewing a family member in this new way may open up the possibility of seeing the authentic essence of this person in a way you have not before.

Prior to beginning the actual letter writing exercises, I am including a section that I believe provides a deep parallel to family healing. In the model of Kidney Swaps that follow, I hope to open up to you the idea that when we cannot connect directly with a lost family member, if they are no longer with us, or they are otherwise emotionally inaccessible to us, a surrogate letter recipient can be very healing. It may be someone already in our life who has provided many of the same qualities otherwise provided by a family member, and by honoring them, you may in fact be healing both relationships. These are just ideas to consider to help you broaden your idea of who your family really is and the healing that may be possible.

The Kidney Swap and Surrogate Families

In a live-donor practice used increasingly in the U.S. over the past few years, a patient who needs a kidney is matched up with a compatible stranger; in return, the patient must line up a friend or relative willing to donate an organ to a stranger, too.

The practice is particularly useful in cases where a kidney patient's friends or relatives are willing to donate an organ to their loved one but are not a suitable match.

In the first U.S. success-rate study of what are called "kidney paired donations," Johns Hopkins University researchers tracked 22 patients who received kidneys from living strangers.

Associated Press, October 4, 2005

I first learned about kidney swaps about two years ago — in a story on CNN. The story presented two families, each of whom had a member who desperately needed a kidney. For each person in need of a kidney, another family member was also willing to provide one. The problem was that the recipients and willing family member were not a direct match. Because of their different blood types, the donation was not possible.

Researchers began to explore the idea that, somewhere, some other family was in the same predicament. Perhaps this other family had the matching blood type to allow the donation to take place.

By honoring the intention of each family member who was willing to donate a kidney to a loved one, the medical researchers used database matching to pair each family with another who could provide the inverse blood type match. Each family would agree to provide a kidney to the other, all in the name of love. The procedure was done with such respect and sensitivity that the two transplant operations were timed within minutes of each other, even if in different physical locations. The donors and recipients were questioned up until the very last minute to ensure that everyone was "still in."

What was particularly moving to me about the model was how family members were so willing to give a physical part of themselves to someone they loved — even if it posed a risk to their own health.

Like the innate urge to give that can be observed in those who have devoted their lives to the emergency service profession, such as firefighters or emergency medical technicians, there is something profound about our willingness to sacrifice ourselves for someone we love. Or in the case of an emergency worker, even someone we don't know.

As I considered this brilliant yet heartfelt model of kidney swapping, I began to contemplate how such a model could be applied to family healing. How many unsuccessful conversations have we had with our mother or father, insisting that they understand us, who we are and the events that have affected our lives? How many times have we demanded that they forgive us or that they apologize and ask for *our* forgiveness in light of events that have gone unresolved in our lives?

What would happen if, on the other hand, we were able to find another human being who had a similar life experiences but sat on the other side of the fence — maybe a mother or father whose actions had left their own child with a similar sense of perceived hurt? How could an interaction with this person change the way we see our own mother or father?

The exercises presented in this section of the book are based around letters of love, honesty, and forgiveness. One model through which theseletter writing exercises can be used is to have them created and read allowed in the presence of *others*, witnesses to our truest self. When the sharing of such a letter with its actual intended recipient may not be comfortable, the act of sharing thoughts and intentions with a surrogate family member can be a deeply healing experience for both people.

I encourage you to explore these letters and even if you do *not* feel comfortable sharing them with their intended recipient, consider sharing them with someone else who may appreciate them. This act may in fact reverberate not only back to your own heart but may allow you to experience other family members, possibly the intended recipient of your love letter, in a completely different light.

The sharing of such a letter in the wrong context or at the wrong time may not lead to the healing and love that was intended from it. It may, in fact, be rejected by the recipient the same way an organ would be rejected by someone with the wrong blood type. Imagine yourself as the kidney donor and how wonderful it is that you have reached this place where you are so willing to give of yourself in this way. Take great pride in this accomplishment for you have come a long way and the fact that you are now engaging in this process of forgiveness and willing to document it by sharing yourself in these letters is an amazing thing.

By taking the metaphor of the kidney swap and applying it to ways in which we can find surrogacy in our transactions of healing and forgiveness, we can reset the course not only of ourselves but of our family as well. The prodigal father wears many faces. As we are willing to recognize him in the many places he may appear to us, we can begin our return home.

Exercises in Writing Love Letters

The letter templates presented in this chapter have been specifically written to be *loving* and not to engage the recipient in a defensive reaction. Your goal is to find the crack under the door or in the window where they can hear you. You'll want to make the letter as loving as possible, while still recognizing your responsibility to share your *gift*, the gift of the truth.

Letters, unlike email and phone calls, naturally belong to the way of love. Letters not only take time to arrive but also take time for you to write and address. They require you to purchase a nice note card or stationary —implying thoughtfulness. I highly recommend that *all* correspondence in this first phase of reaching out involve real letters in the mail. Although it is completely appropriate once you have change in a relationship to communicate regularly via email or phone, it is not recommended as a starting point.

As previously discussed, family relationships can carry generations of unconscious trauma and neglect. Because we are so "comfortable" with one another, our expectation is that we can unload on one another, behave poorly, and mistreat one another all within what has become an almost socially acceptable model of family behavior. With everyone in a family subscribing to this belief, there is little room left for giving, let alone places or spaces for one to find and be one's authentic self.

So imagine, if you will, that you are approaching the members of your family in a new way. You open your mind to the following concepts:

Like you, this family member endured deep trauma that has most likely never been either recognized or processed. There have been moments along her own journey at which she may have been able to recognize where her path was altered — her spirit muted.

Like you, this family member has an authentic self that has for the most part gone unrecognized. He may very well be eager to share but be willing to do only in *a safe emotional space*. This requires an enormous amount of reframing within the context of your relationship. A "love letter" would be a great place to start.

Most likely, the more splintered the relationship with this family member, the more of your protective selves each of you has enlisted in your relationship. There is probably a significant set of events that have deeply hurt both of you, possibly in different ways, and your relationship may have become *simpatico* in the mutual protection against revisiting these events and possibly being reinjured by them.

Once you have recognized this, you may have to hold firm in your recognition of this in the presence of the other person. Some of the most charged and difficult relationships in families are among siblings, because siblings carry *matching* energy fields — like two negative or positive magnets that naturally pull and repel from each other.

In writing the letters, you may want to start with the easiest, perhaps a letter to a cousin. This is similar to the way a gardener trims the most outer branches of the tree first — giving it more room to grow and allowing the healthy parts of the tree more access to sunlight.

You can then work your way to family members who are closer to you — the "heart" so to speak — but know that this is where you will most likely meet the most resistance within yourself. Where the trunk of the tree meets its closest, oldest and most permanent "offspring" branches, the trunk is thick and less flexible. Making changes in this part of the tree can take years, but that should not discourage you from beginning your efforts.

A Letter to My Spouse

We are often so caught up in taking care of one another as a married couple (and of our children as co-parents) that we forget the special qualities that attracted us to one another prior to becoming man and wife.

As my friend Elyse once asked jokingly, "Why don't we just seek out someone we are really good at bickering with, someone who really gets on our nerves and manages to put down everything we do — and marry them?"

With all of the work that being married and managing a family requires, it is so important to remember to keep alive the gifts we have found in being together. Writing letters and notes to each other, even on non-special occasions, can be a wonderful way to say *thank you* to each other just for being in each other's lives.

Rich and I have a stack of notes and cards we have written to one another from when we first met as well as from times when we've had very rough disagreements. As I look back at these letters, I have noticed some common themes that might be useful as you consider a letter to your spouse:

1. ## *What I admire about him or her*
   It is always a good starting point to begin with what you most admire about your spouse. First, it sets the tone for the note or letter as loving and positive. Second, it reminds *you* of what you truly love about your spouse and invites into your letter room for *grace* to lift whatever resentment or frustration you may be harboring about your spouse.

2. ## *An example of this quality in action*
   Often the act of recalling a story from the past when your spouse has exhibited great courage or thoughtfulness helps refocus you on the gifts that your spouse brings to your and your family's life. If the example includes other family members or close friends — even better. We must recognize our appreciation for one another in moments when he or she has exhibited great examples of kindness — especially in

situations that are emotionally challenging. These are special moments to remember and acknowledge in our spouse.

3. *A challenging moment for you in his or her presence*
Common practices in marriage therapy teach us to steer clear of the *you* word. It can appear threatening when you accuse someone of something you believe they have done. But more important, it gives them the other person illusionary and unreal power over your own peace of mind. To believe that your happiness is dependent on someone else's behavior is a slippery slope and one that assigns both parties a false sense of power. When we acknowledge that a particular *moment* in the presence of another human being is challenging for us, we can explore *why* this is challenging for us and how we can see both these moments *and* this person differently. For example, you may discover that it is hard for you to be around your spouse when he or she complains. Instead of accusing him of this, look into your own heart and trace the events in your life that might have made words of disappointment trigger points for you. By exploring, sharing, and owning these reactions, you continue the lifelong process of getting to know your spouse and yourself, as well as free him or her from the false responsibility of managing your moods and state of mind.

4. *Tell something you are looking forward to sharing together in the future*
Elvis Presley once said that happiness means having someone to love, something to do, and something to look forward to. When we can remember that we are two separate individuals on a very adventurous journey together, we can maintain a sense of wonder and excitement about our marriage. Keeping something special that we have planned to do together in the forefront of our hearts can keep us connected through what might feel like very difficult or unconnected times. It may even be something we do routinely, like getting coffee a certain morning of the week, or a walk or a trip to the store. But by acknowledging that you are looking forward to it, you

elevate the sacredness of your time together to a more loving and positive place.

Finally, a word about the frequency and rituals of writing letters to one another. We may scribe a birthday, valentine, or maybe even holiday card to our spouse, but after years of marriage it may not be so eloquent or prolific. Consider how moving it would be to get a card that honors and remembers the parts of your spirit you continue to share with one another in your journey. Putting these feelings and thoughts onto paper and sharing them with your spouse can be a gift beyond anything purchased from the jewelry store.

You may decide that there are special dates that you share, such as when you first met, or the birth of your children, that trigger warm and loving feelings for one another. The more of these dates you can recognize, the more you can create a calendar full of rituals of love that break up the patterns of the stressful work week or monotonous months in your life.

Love letters to one another can be particularly powerful for spouses or partners who must spend time apart on a regular basis. I was told once by a marriage counselor that couples who are apart for more than three days a week on a regular basis may be prone to losing touch with one another, and that the absentee spouse may lose touch with the family altogether. By committing to sharing these heartfelt messages with one another on a regular basis, you may find that the lonely places in your day, night, or even week will feel less lonely. This period may be remembered one day as a special time when you had the opportunity to share parts of yourself with each other that you might have otherwise not known.

A Letter to My Mother / Father

You would be surprised to know how important letters from grown children are to their parents. Gone from the house and entering into your own life and reality, you may have less time to think about or interact with your parents on a regular basis. Even where a parent and child relationship is strained, there are great opportunities for healing in writing love letters to your parents.

Children usually carry a far deeper intuitive imprint of their parents than the other way around. As parents, we see our babies born and have a deep sense of their original nature and essence. But over time, the stresses of raising a family and trying to make all of the personalities in the family "mesh" can lead us to project issues from our own pasts onto our children, as well as to mute out the qualities they carry that we cannot relate to or find irritating.

As grown children, many of us carry a mental file cabinet of experiences with our parents. We have filed away many memories of them finding frustration with us or of losing their temper at us. Or maybe we simply remember our parents as less than happy and felt helpless about this.

But the truly beautiful thing about the parent-child bond is that children will always naturally long for a chance to forgive and re-bond with a lost parent. When we share love letters with our parents, we *invite* opportunities for just such an interaction. By releasing our parents of this guilt, we allow them to reclaim it and in turn release it from within themselves.

When writing a letter to a lost parent or even a parent you love dearly but have become disconnected from even temporarily, include some of the following points:

1. *Thanking your mother or father for their gifts*

    Our parents may have fallen short in many ways in raising us, or at least of our expectations of raising us, but we can usually find gifts that they have given us along the way. In writing a love letter to your mother or father, a "Thank you" for even one of these gifts is a wonderful place to start. If we are going through a particularly angry phase with a parent, this can prove to be very healing — inviting grace to help us let go of

101

the interaction with our parent that has triggered a state of anger or protection in us. The gift may have been their support for us in something we eventually became very good at or that fostered our artistic or musical talents. It may have been a special time they spent with us, separate from the rest of the family, or even a moment when they helped us see something in our lives differently. If nothing else, you can simply thank your mother or father for bringing you into the world.

2. *Something you and your parent have in common and why this has been a gift for you*
Those of us who were raised in traumatic or stressful households spend a lot of time — once we make the move from our childhood home to our adult home —making mental lists of how we are *not like* our parents, how we will *not be like* our parents, and ways we can live our lives to maintain a separate existence that will prevent us from recreating the patterns we have seen in our own childhood home.

As we age, however, we begin to tear down this imposed separation, facing the reality that our parents' moods, ways, and habits have found their way into our own ways of being. It may not have been our plan, or even what we hoped for, but ultimately we are the bearers of the torch of our family legacy, the keepers of the bad code.

Acknowledging that we, too, are burdened with some of these difficult traits and life challenges — challenges that keep us from living more fully, loving more completely, and keeping a union with our truer self — is a great gift for our parents to see. Our parents may be saddened to learn that we, too, carry the burden of the decades of family experiences, but a part of them will be relieved to know that we can clearly see this part of ourselves and accept it both within ourselves and in them.

By acknowledging that we have a shared issue, such as our anxiety at certain types of events or our tendency to lose our temper when we become frightened or scared, we let our parents know that these moments in life, these traits, are not insurmountable. By talking with your parent about the shared quality or trait and how you have found your way through this will provide your parent with hope on many levels.

3. Share something with your mother or father they may not know about you

One of the statements I hear again and again from people when they talk about their frustration with their parents is that their parents *don't get them*. There are whole aspects of their personalities that they feel go completely overlooked. Endless movies and stories have been written about the grown adult who comes home for the holidays and tries to share some newly realized aspect of her personality, only to be reminded of some shortcoming she had when she was fourteen.

Letter writing is a wonderful format for sharing these parts of yourself and your life with your parents. Because the format of letter writing lends itself to story telling, it gives you an open format to share aspects of yourself since you have left home.

When writing these stories, be aware of how you present them and the left-brain critical messages that come up while you are sharing. We are not setting out here to win our parents' approval; when we write letters with that as our primary intention, we may miss a unique opportunity to be genuine with them. When we can be truly genuine with our parents, even in writing, we set an example that can greatly benefit our parents. Despite the pain our parents may have caused us, they find peace in knowing that we know they love us. When we can share ourselves freely without fear of judgment or with the agenda of approval, we provide them with this gift.

4. Tell me more about you

When our parents brought us into the world, they may have been children themselves. We were so small and they were so big. Despite the volumes of stories and images we had of them while we were growing up, we did not have access to what they were dealing with before we were born or when they left the room or the house and went into the world. As we grow to the ages our parents were at the time of our clearest memories of them, we may gain new appreciation for what they, too, may have been going through.

By understanding that we, in fact, do not know it all, but only a piece of the story, we find a new way to respect our parents' unique reality. A wonderful way to honor this is to ask your mother or father exactly what it was that made a particular life moment difficult for them. You may find a way to relate it to a similar experience that you have had or are having in your own parenting journey.

We often underestimate how much our parents loved us and what a great divide there was between what they had hoped for us and what they could deliver. Asking them to share what was behind the limited delivery opens the door for them to share the love and plans that may have been lost along the way.

A Letter to My Son / Daughter

For any parent who feels they were not able to give their child the love or nurturing they had hoped to provide as a parent, a love letter offers great opportunities for healing and moving forward.

There are two very important and basic messages you can continue to give your children as they grow (or even if they are already grown). They include, most importantly, humility and recognition. Here are some thoughts on how to share these feelings:

1. *Stories of humility*

    Love letters to your grown children, or even your young children, are a unique opportunity to provide them with the greatest gift you could possibly give— the gift of humility.

    In sharing moments of humility with your children, you continue to reinforce not only your love for them, but their ability to practice *being more loving toward themselves*. As they see you practice the art of forgiveness, they learn how capable you are of change, of letting the past roll into the past, and making way and room for more loving and respectful ways of being.

    A word on sharing stories of humility with your children: The more specific you can be the better. It will be tempting to say to your child, "I am sorry for all the times I was not there for you, or for when I ignored you, or just wasn't a very good mother or father." This does not really create room for either of you to grow, as it simply states a vague idea that may represent a different experience for each of you. When, however, you can be very specific about an event and share the moment, what happened, what you did wrong, how you would do it differently today, and why you know that this is something you must change, you will strike a chord with your child. You allow him, too, to send this moment into the past, as well as feel hopeful about his own ability to forgive himself should he be met with similar challenges in life.

2. *Offer deep and specific recognition*

The beauty of our children always being our children is that, as their parents, we will never be fired from the role of "ultimate compliment giver." However old we may be, we know that to receive recognition from our parents brings deep pride to both of us. When a child is born, we cannot help but look into her face and see perfection and beauty. In that moment, we commit ourselves to keeping that perfection and beauty in her face for as long as possible and to supporting her in her sharing of her unique grace and beauty with the world. Noticing specific things our children have done — especially acts that reflect the qualities they particularly value and have spent great time cultivating in themselves — is one of the deepest and truest bonds we can share with them as a parent.

3. *Setting them free of just ONE of the critical voices*

There are most likely repetitive patterns in your relationship with your son or daughter that have in your child's mind become rivers of self-criticism. They may be things you have nagged them about over the years, things that may seem simple and easy to fix to you, but for whatever reason, have remained challenging to your child.

More than likely, your child carries deep scars around these issues and the legacy of criticism you have left them with. If you have the opportunity, think of some stride, small or great, that they have made and point this out to them. This is a chance to undo the criticism and replace it with real recognition, helping to free them of the constant struggle that they undoubtedly live with.

Remember, if you show your child that you believe in him, that you know he is capable of overcoming even the things that *you* fear they are *not*, you create a space for healing that you can both benefit from!

The beauty of the parent-child relationship is its continued calling for and acceptance of forgiveness and love. Regardless of the pain that has transpired in this relationship, there is nothing more lovely than the reconciliation between a parent and a child. The reality of this experience requires great humility and insight from

106

both the parent *and* the child. *Our letters to our children and our own ability to share our humility in the face of our wrongdoings is a profound step in this healing process.*

A Letter to My Brother / Sister

As we discussed earlier, sibling bonds can become particularly overloaded with repelling and magnetic energy because siblings are deeply embedded in the triangle with our parents.

The proliferation of old memories between two siblings can take on a life of its own — deeply reverberating displaced energy handed down through generations in a family can create an infinite loop of wounds between these two souls.

A letter to your sibling may be the hardest and even trickiest of all. You may find yourself called by your mother or father (or if the relationships are really sophisticated, even a third sibling) to pull away from attempts at healing in this arena, as you may believe them to be too dangerous.

However, the exercise of writing this letter will be useful for these very reasons. I share with you specifics on what to say in this letter, but another level of exercise is recommended as well. While you are writing this letter, imagine, if you will, at every word or sentence *who* in your family is over your shoulder at that moment, engaging with you and what they are trying to interject

This exercise has in it the promise of debunking the triangle formation in your sibling relationship — allowing you to see more clearly who else is participating in this relationship *you thought* you were having *just* with your sibling.

When composing a letter to a sibling, especially a sibling with whom you have experienced great tension, jealousy, or resentment, consider the inclusion of the following points:

1. *What makes your sibling unique*
   First and foremost, when we start a reconciliatory dialogue with an estranged or lost sibling, we must begin with something they most likely did not receive from your parents: a respect and honor of their uniqueness. I can put my money down that if you are not talking to her, if you have had a falling out, one or both of you got lost in the early years. Both

107

your truest essence were either muted or lost in a constant competition with you or another sibling.

Find something special about this sibling, something you know inside your heart has been for years overlooked about him and offer him the gift of recognition. The more specific you can be the better. He may have had a great success that he feels he was never fully congratulated on, or a life downfall or tragedy such as a divorce or a lost child. For whatever reasons, "the family" was not able to properly honor this event. Recognize this event and his unique qualities in how he handled it.

2. *Share a vulnerability of your own*

   This may well be one of the most difficult things in all the exercises in this book, but it will forever register with your sibling as a message that you are willing to put down the competitive sword and be real with her. If you can share with her a story that illustrates how you have dealt with a shortcoming, you invite them to be honest as well. You may even find that this trait of yours is not something they share and that they can offer you new insights into this issue. The key to this sharing, however, is that you show them that you, too, are human, have suffered as they have, and are willing to share this.

3. *A simple omission*

   If you are aware of a specific difficulty that your sibling endured as a result of you just being alive, share with them an acknowledgment of this. Because so much of sibling rivalry has little to do with the actual interactions of siblings, it can be very powerful simply to acknowledge where that jealousy stems from. You may have had a closer relationship with a parent than they did, more access to a parent's time, more resources available to you (better schools, lessons, clothes). By acknowledging this, you debunk and demystify much of what has probably kept you separate all these years. This act is very powerful and may require that you look a little deeper in a nonattached, empathetic way at their lives.

4. The party in the house

Last, I recommend that you point out to your sibling that, although the two of you have had great moments together, many other potential good moments have been sucked away in the black hole of your family's bad code. This is in no way intended to be a gripe session or a chance to slam your parents. It is an acknowledgment of what all siblings are entitled to but few receive: a chance to have their true essence honored not only by their parents, but by each other.

There are so many unspoken words and spirits that live in the relationship; you may find it the most daunting relationship of all to heal. Remember, however, the power of one healed sibling bond. It can reverberate out to the rest of the family, the triangles, the future generations, and create a playground of family love that carries far into old age, restoring our youth in ways we cannot even imagine. Our sibling bonds will forever keep us young. Take the time to honor and recognize those parts of your sibling that no one else in the family could see. It may be one of the most rewarding exercises of time you can engage in.

Letters to Extended Family

We can write letters to our mothers and fathers, our children, and even to our siblings. But an often overlooked opportunity for healing lies in our ability to share our own lives with lost relatives.

We may have an aunt, grandparent, or cousin who knew us and had a deep fondness for us, but due to our family strife, we have lost contact with them. We do well to remember them and the impression we left on their lives. Knowing that we are okay today and creating joy and happiness for ourselves and our growing family could be deeply healing for them.

Letters to extended family usually do not require so much care in stepping through post-traumatic stress mind fields. They may be wonderful opportunities to share the great successes and moments of joy we have experienced and are experiencing in our present life.

If you are not a grandparent or aunt or uncle now, you may well be one day, and you will understand the importance of these gestures. Letters from a younger generation, especially hand-written notes, cards and photographs, offer hope that the disappointments of the past may be finally replaced with a new enthusiasm for life.

A Letter to My Former Husband / Wife

An often underrated but extremely powerful reconciliation in the family fabric is that between a former husband and wife. Although it may seem like a tall order, a letter to your former husband or wife, at any passage, has great healing implications for the entire family, especially when the burdens of this break-up of the marriage have been carried by its children.

If communications with a former spouse are strained, the efforts to write this letter will be great. I am very familiar with the pains of divorce, having watched my own parents, other relatives, and close friends go through it. Strife from a broken marriage comes from a wound that has not yet been healed with the ointment of forgiveness. The forgiveness ointment must first be applied to your own heart, *and then and only then* can it be applied to the former spouse.

When you look at the wrongs that were done to you in your marriage and see only blame with your partner, you are probably not looking deep enough. If it were that simple, if *they* simply did something wrong, you would most likely have recognized it in that moment and set the relationship on the appropriate course. You would probably not be in the place of pain you are in today.

Most likely, the events or behaviors that led to your separation took place over years, and were repeated again and again. You likely built up not only anger at your former spouse, but bitterness toward *yourself* for continuing to let these things happen.

And so, as strange as this may sound, I recommend that before writing a letter of forgiveness to your former spouse, you write a longer letter of forgiveness *to yourself.* The letter does not need to cover everything; it just needs to look at one single aspect of your marriage that was hard for you to come to terms with — perhaps an aspect that you believe you tolerated for far too long and have never really forgiven yourself for.

Taking a page from *The Work* by Byron Katie, I encourage you to jump right to what Katie refers to as "the turnaround." The turn around refers to taking some thought or feeling that holds you prisoner and turning it around on its head — looking at it from a new perspective. Try presenting the turnaround in a letter to yourself:

Dear (Me),

1. **I recognize that in my marriage to (your former spouse), I continually LET him (or her) hurt me in the following ways.**

    List one or more specific things that you feel your spouse did to hurt you. Go into as much detail as you would like. You may find this exercise very healing as it provides you with a great amount of freedom in finally saying things on paper you may have only said before in your mind or with a close friend. Getting them out of your body onto paper can actually change the physical make-up of these thoughts and feelings in your body.

    Acknowledging the turnaround here admits that the hurt was not done to you but rather allowed by you. Although this is a frightening place to go, it gives you a chance to forgive yourself and regain a sense of control over your own destiny. You free yourself from the illusion that you are a victim of someone else's behavior and are an active participant in the events of your life.

2. **Acknowledge to yourself that you did only what you were capable of doing in each of these moments as the perceived hurt was accumulating.**

    This is a *key* step in your own forgiveness process. You must acknowledge that, as they say, if you knew better, you would have done better. You, like many others in such paralyzing and painful moments, did all you could to hold on to your sanity and hold onto the little place inside of yourself you needed to just to survive in light of the mounting confusion and pain.

3. **Recognize and understand that when you were gifted with a new perspective on how to deal with this old situation in a new way, your life and the marriage were forever changed.**

    By honoring this transition, we also accept that life is full of grace, and answers, solutions and new ways of seeing life are often gifted to us in their own time. No matter how hard we push, we cannot always find our way to this new place on our own time schedule. Be thankful for the gift of grace and for its ability to release you from the role of God and from the false belief that you control everything, including your own ability to behave differently in the presence of the person you have always been.

After completing this letter to yourself, take it as you would a letter to anyone else you care about and spend the less than half a dollar to put it in the mail and mail it to yourself. In the day or so you wait patiently for the letter of forgiveness to yourself, you will feel the new forgiveness washing over you and will have a chance to start to imagine what this forgiveness feels like.

By the time you receive this letter and read it to yourself, hopefully in a quiet place in your home, you may begin to see that your former spouse is not a whole lot different from you in his or her inability to do or act differently without the divine intervention of grace.

Should you so feel inspired, write the same letter with the steps I have recommended above except this time, make the recipient of your letter and the forgiveness your former spouse, acknowledging the perceived actions of hurt and also acknowledging that had *they* known better, they *also* would have done better.

Love Letters in Our Daily Lives

As you explore these exercises in love letter writing, you will begin to feel the power of sharing in this way from your heart. I often recommend creating a special love letter box in your home, somewhere accessible where you can access these tools when you are sitting, watching TV, thinking or have a free moment. Also in this box, keep a birthday and anniversary calendar to remind you of all of the people in your life, the tree and circles of your family and the celebratory occasions that have been a part of its continued growth.

If you can integrate this process of love letter writing into your regular life, even making an intention to always honor birthdays and anniversaries even with a simple card, your love and efforts of healing will echo into both the generations of the past as well as forward into the future in ways you may not even appreciate or see the fruits of in this lifetime.

Letter writing has become a lost art and yet its power has not faded. When we can put our feelings and our love into words and send them off on real pieces of paper into corners of the world and our family tree, we can provide sunlight and water in places that may have remained dark and thirsty for years gone by.

Conclusion

When you realize where you came from,
You naturally become tolerant,
Disinterested, amused,
Kindhearted as a grandmother,
Dignified as a king.
- Lao Tzu, Tao Te Ching - Stephen Mitchell translation

As we revisit the story of the prodigal son, we are reacquainted with the ingredients of family reconciliation (separation, transformation, reintegration) and the magic ingredients of humility and forgiveness. The story of the prodigal son is the story of the archetypal hero, the lost children, and all parents who sit in longful waiting for their child's return home. There are many aspects to this story that resonate true to the wounded family, lost adolescence, and the hopeful and final act of growing up.

There are many colors and nuances to the prodigal son's story that reflect chapters in our collective family stories. Not everyone born under the same roof receives the nurturing he needs to develop his most true self. The reason for this may not even be due to neglect or abuse, or any kind of malice. The reason may simply be that a particular soul born into a family may be called to a journey that takes them outside their family, often even at an inconvenient time. The purpose of such a calling and its eventual journey may not be realized for years or decades to come.

The prodigal son left his home for reasons even he could not understand in the moment. The path he thought he was taking, that of a life of quick ease and pleasure, turned out to be nothing of what he eventually found within the world and himself. The message behind such a journey is that we must trust our calling to somewhere and something different, despite the social taboos that might surround such a separation. It is a lesson primarily in trust and in believing in the intervention of grace to take us to a new place — a place that would have remained unknown to us had we not answered the call to find a life beyond our family.

The relationship between the prodigal son and his brother offers insight into another very important yet misunderstood lost family relationship — that of jealous siblings. While many archetypal stories have focused on the bond between mother and child and even father and son, few have recognized the lost gifts that exist between two siblings, caught in the parallel yet different worlds of how they have experienced the same upbringing in vastly different ways and the resentment that sits between them.

Last I would say that the ultimate coming home may not resemble the return of the prodigal son to his father in a literal sense — but may present itself in hidden forms over and over in our lives. We may not return to our own parents and to their welcoming arms when we are finally reunited with our truest self. But the form of the prodigal father and his display of forgiveness and acceptance may take many other shapes in our life especially if we are willing to be open to this love and acceptance in other people and other experiences — others that may come to us as angels in our lives in the forms of teachers, friends, distant relatives, coworkers and even neighbors. When we are willing to accept that our real family may not be confined to the bloodlines of our original family tree, we can rebuild our family circles in new ways and create new family vines that resemble the grafted apple tree, giving our new generation nurturing and hope beyond what may have been previously possible.

Not all of us will experience our most challenging moments in life trying to make sense of our place within our family. But for those of us who do, what answering the call of such a journey may require of you may at first feel unnatural. As we accept the challenge of being willing to step back and look at not only our own shadow, but the collective shadow of our family and even our ancestors, we allow ourselves the freedom to finally pass through the cycle of a true adolescent journey and to grow up and become the person we were destined to be.

What we will inevitably realize on this journey is that the only way *through* such a passage is by not only *healing around that which cannot be healed*, but also learning to *embrace, honor and mourn* that which cannot be healed, understanding that it has in fact been passed down through many generations and most likely has its original roots in a set of collective social events that were not even related to our family, its personalities or the abilities of any individual to nurture his or her children.

By learning to recognize that we are in fact part of a larger social structure and that our family life is not immune to the changes

116

in the ecosystem of the culture and historical circumstances in which it exists is to create the space for forgiveness of these ancestral truths and let them go for once and for all. True maturity can only be realized when we are no longer the child in our relationships even with our parents, but come to see them with the same love and compassion we see ourselves and even our own children. This is the true crossing over of the hero's journey as it relates to our relationship with our family story, where we and we alone can bring back our gift to our family and share the fruits of our work on our journey as the deepest contribution we can make to both our ancestors and our children.

As I revisit the story of the prodigal son, I continue to find comfort in the fact that there can be no passage through adolescence without a true and honest separation from the family story that has tied us to a false sense of ourselves. We must leave the house of our father, even if that house is just the voices we carry at forty-five years old in our mind, and finally venture out to find out who we are in relation to the world and allow ourselves to have the union with our true self that we can then bring home. Who is there to greet us may not be who we expect, and we must remember that even our parents may not have had the space and freedom to take this journey and so then it is all we can do to forgive them for not being who we thought they should have been but instead remember that they may one day come knocking from their own journey, and we will be truly healed if we are ready to greet them and celebrate *their* return with the feast of the fattened pig.

More than ever, our Earth is in need of her children to take the needed journey and become grownups. We can begin to understand the importance of this when we feel our circles closing in and have little emotional space to let our own children grow and find their way. By staying honest and open to these important truths, without judgment, we can begin to create new code where we can live a more loving and peaceful life, both inside and outside the space we call home.

Appendix: References and Recommended Reading

A Course in Miracles, Dr. Helen Schucman - Foundation for Inner Peace

How Good Do we Have to Be, Harold S. Kushner - Back Bay Books

Five Things we Cannot Change, David Richo - Shambhala

Lessons in Loving, David Robert Ord - Namaste

Living Dialogues (audio interview series), with Duncan Campbell

Loving What Is, Byron Katie - Three Rivers Press

Negotiation Generation, Lynne Reeves Griffin - Berkley Trade

Reflections on the Art of Living: A Joseph Campbell Companion, Diane K. Osbon - Harper Perennial

Screamfree Parenting, Hal Edward Runkel - Broadway

Self Esteem (Audio), Carolyn Myss - Playaway

Siblings without Rivalry, Adele Faber and Elaine Mazlish – Harper Paperbacks

Soul Mates, Thomas Moore - Harper Perennial

Soulshaping, Jeff brown - North Atlantic Books

Tao Te Ching, Lau Tzu – Translation by Steven Mitchell - Harper Perennial Modern Classics

The Bowen Center (Murray Bowen) – www.thebowencenter.org

The Catholic Study Bible - Oxford University Press

The Four Agreements, Don Miguel Ruiz - Amber-Allen Publishing

The Four Fold Way, Angeles Arienn - HarperOne

The Drama of the Gifted Child, Alice Miller – Basic Books

The Goddess and the Alphabet , Leonard Shlain - Penguin

The Passionate Marriage, David Schnarch - W.W. Norton & Co.;

The Power of Myth, Joseph Campbell - Anchor

The Prophet, Kahlil Gibran - Alfred A. Knopf

The Revolutionary Trauma Release Process, David Berceli - Namaste

The Twelve Conditions of a Miracle, Todd Michael - Tarcher

The Unexpected Legacy of Divorce, Judith Wallenstein - Hyperion

About the Author

After undergoing treatment for breast cancer at forty-two, Johanna Maaghul's path was permanently altered. As an important part of her healing process she began to look closely at her own family story and ask the question, why do so many family relationships break down and how can they be reconciled? The Prodigal Family provides her own unique perspective on this ancient question. Johanna lives in northern California with her husband and three children.

Made in the USA
Lexington, KY
14 June 2015